LIFE'S A HOOT

MEMOIRS OF A
TV NEWS JOURNALIST

GENE HUNTER

authorHOUSE®

AuthorHouse™
1663 Liberty Drive
Bloomington, IN 47403
www.authorhouse.com
Phone: 1 (800) 839-8640

Published by AuthorHouse 06/17/2019

ISBN: 978-1-7283-1548-5 (sc)
ISBN: 978-1-7283-1547-8 (hc)
ISBN: 978-1-7283-1546-1 (e)

Library of Congress Control Number: 2019907471

Print information available on the last page.

CONTENTS

With sincere appreciation to my son Michael who so graciously provided his infinite computer knowledge and very limited time in making this effort possible. To my beloved daugher-in-law, Tracy, for her inestimable help in bringing this book to its conclusion. Also, to my niece Bonae Scholl, who unknowingly inspired this book as well as my first" A Cowboy's Midnight Poems"

To all my friends and family for their love and support, I humbly dedicate this book.

ABOUT THE AUTHOR

Born in Mebane, North Carolina, Gene Hunter was raised in nearby Burlington. Gene was an only child whose father was killed on Iwo Jima.

A graduate of Williams High School, he attended East Carolina University. After a college job in radio, he entered the Air Force, where he continued his broadcasting career on Armed Forces radio.

Four years later, he returned home, and went to work in radio and television. Gene spent the next fifteen years in broadcast journalism. He was Capitol Correspondent for WRAL-TV in Raleigh and News Director for WITN-TV in Washington, North Carolina.

Gene was married to the love of his life for 40 years. Together they raised 4 children.

He is a Mason, and enjoys writing, painting, gardening, horseback riding and reading.

A lifetime of farming, raising horses and kids, along with 20 years in the broadcast business, he has garnered some amusing tales.

The collections of stories in this book are accurate to the best of his ability to remember them.

FOREWORD

I am beginning this book on September 20th, 2016, my 79th birthday and feel at this age, I better hurry. Hopefully, with the help of God, I will retain my clear thoughts until I can get it completed. My trip through life has, like most people, not been without its problems. But it has also been a hoot, to say the least. I will endeavor not to dwell on the sad times. As Marjorie Hinkley said "The only way to get through life is to laugh your way through it. You either have to laugh or cry. I prefer to laugh. Crying gives me a headache." After being on this earth for the better part of a century, I feel my stories are worth sharing. And after that many years of living, I should have no problem filling a book.

My first book, "A Cowboys Midnight Poems" consisted of twelve years of poetry. So, I guess this book may be considered poetic justice. OK folks, Tim Conway I'm not. If you enjoy the read, it will be an effort well spent. I hope it will be a great legacy for my family as well as an insight into their father's life.

In your travels with me through through the pages of my life, we will cover some of history's greatest moments as well as some of my funniest. You will quickly see that there is a focus on my "loves" in every part of my life: broadcasting, horses, poetry, art and most of all, my family. I claim no greatness in any of these areas, just a love for them all. You will come to the realization that every goal I set, large or small, I eventually achieved. I stress, these achievements were my goals, not anyone's expectations of my goals.

All my life, I have only been willing to give life what I wanted it to have and remain a contented person. Never have I entertained even the slightest notion of giving life what it expected of me. While it is important what people think of me, it did not define me. Some people are willing to give up everything to reach a certain status quo and to me that is unthinkable. Society refers to it as paying the price. Regardless of what the world thought, as "Ole Blue Eyes", Frank Sinatra sang, "I did it my way". My peace of mind, happiness, and contentment was always foremost in my mind. I read where the world resists your notions and ideas until you convince it of the finality of it, and then it falls in line and supports you. When I reached a certain point in life where the circumstances were dictating my peace of mind, I changed the equation. I realized early on that for me to make others happy, I had to be happy. I feel so many people either can't or don't figure that out until it's too late.

I have worked at several radio and television stations. In those moves, I went from Reporter to State Capital Correspondent to Assignment Editor. Eventually, I went to News Editor, Anchorman and News Director. The next progression was to network news, and while it's every newsmans ambition, leaving my great rural life and moving my famiily to a big city was not in the cards. No regrets ever. Oh! I'm human folks. I toyed with the idea, even to the point of discussing it, on several occasions, with the network editors. My salary would have been ten times what I was making at the time. But I would take that long country road back to the beautiful rolling hills of Snow Camp, North Carolina, lovingly referred to as God's country, and I would snap back to the reality of what I would have to give up. It was the devil's bargain. Just one example of what life expected from me and one that I wasn't willing to give up.

While income was important to the welfare of my family and eventually became the reason I left the business I loved, it never became the most important aspect of my life. Over the years, I have probably given away as much as money I have kept. As the saying goes "You can't outgive God". And every penny I gave away was the best money I ever spent.

Henry David Thoreau wrote "Why should we be in such desperate haste to succeed and in such desperate enterprises? If a man does not keep pace with his companions, perhaps it is because he hears the beat of a different drummer. Let him step to the music which he hears, however measured or far away".

ATTITUDE

The longer I live, the more I realize the impact of attitude on life. Attitude, to me is more important than facts. It is more important than the past, education, money, circumstances, failures, successes, more than what other people think or say or do.

Attitude will make or break a man, woman, church, home, family, or business. The remarkable thing is we have a choice every day regarding the attitude we will embrace for that day.

We cannot change our past, we cannot change the fact that people will act a certain way. We cannot change the inevitable. The only thing we can do is play on the one thing we can control, and that is our attitude.

I am convinced that life is 10% what happened to me and 90% how I reacted to what happened to me. And so it is with you, we are in charge of our attitude.

I hope you enjoy the book. I will vigorously strive not to leave out anything humorous.

Thank you for taking precious minutes from your life to read it. God bless and keep this country great.

ABOUT THE BOOK

"From out of the past come the thundering hoof-beats of the great horse Silver. The Lone Ranger rides again!" booms the voice of the Merita bread announcer on the radio, as the coconut shells make the hoof beat noise on a table in the background. Now, if you remember that phrase then you are old enough to really enjoy this book. We return to the times when a vivid imagination played a very important role in the enjoyment of life and, hopefully, take you back to some of the good times. I have endeavored to cover a lot of monumental incidents as they happened over the years and affected me, and I hope, you as well.

If you are a young person you will learn a lot of history. If older, you will remember quite a bit of it. If a senior, well, more than likely most of it. It's called a lifetime, and though it seems like an eternity when you are young, it is but a fleeting moment on the scales of time.

I have always maintained that if you are writing something; make it interesting enough for people not to have wasted their precious time reading. I sincerely hope that is the case in this endeavor. As you read through this dissertation, I hope you will remind yourself that through all the stresses in daily living, life is still "Just a Hoot". With kindest regards and a good read.

CHAPTER 1

THE FORMIDABLE YEARS

Gene at age 5

WILBUR CALVIN HUNTER

In the beginning… I know that's the way many books start, but let's face it, everything must start somewhere. For me, it was February 23, 1945. I was seven, and we had just been informed that my father was killed in action on Iwo Jima.

Iwo Jima is part of a chain of islands called the Bonin Islands located south of Tokyo, Japan. The Bonin Islands consists of Haha Jima, Chichi Jima, Iwo Jima, O 'Shima, Hachijo Jima And Nii Jima. The Island of Iwo Jima had three airfields and during WWII, the American military looked at it as prime real estate to launch bombing raids against Japan. The takeover of the island of Iwo was expected to take three to four days. Thirty-six days later, Iwo Jima had been secured by our troops. During the Battle of Iwo Jima, 26,000 American troops were injured and 6,800 soldiers lost their lives. My father, Wilber Calvin Hunter, was one of them.

The U.S Military occupied Iwo Jima until 1968 when it returned it to Japan. If you would like to read more on the battle, I suggest the book *The Ghosts of Iwo Jima* by Robert S. Burrell.

I only have one memory of my father. I must have been around 5 or 6 and he was home on furlough after his boot camp training. I remember, he owned an Indian motorcycle, Indian being a forerunner to the Harley Davidson. He sat me in front of him on the gas tank of that Indian and took me for a ride. I thought Mom would have a heart attack, but I was a boy and I loved it! That was his only furlough before heading into combat and it would be the last time I would ever see him.

My mom and I were heading out to a party at my aunt's house when we received the telegram notifying us of his death. Even at that young age, I understood that this single piece of paper would change the trajectory of my life. I cried all the way to my aunt's and all the way home. Losing my father left a hole in my heart and a sadness I had never felt before in my young life.

Later, after art courses in college and while in the military, I sketched my own concept of the raising of the flag on Mt. Suribachi. To this day, some 60 years later, it still hangs in my office at home.

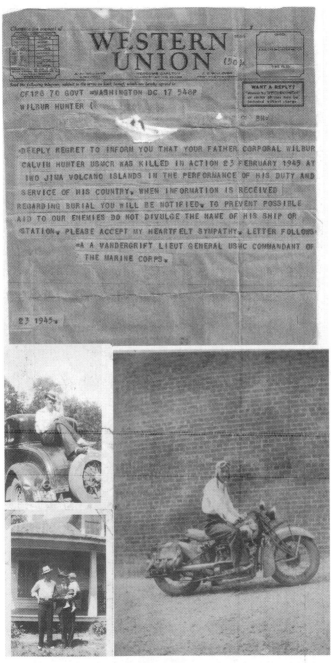

With very few memories of my father, I cherish these – Telegram from War Department, Photo of Wilbur sitting on a car, the motorcycle he took me riding on and a photo of Grandaddy, my father and me.

SIX BOYS THAT BECAME HEROES

Iwo Jima memorial is the largest bronze statue in the world and depicts one of the most famous photographs in military history: Six brave young men raising the American flag about Mount Surabachi on the Iwo Jima in WW II.

The first guy putting the pole in the ground is Harlon Block. an all-state football player. Harlon, died at the age of twenty-one, with his intestines in his hands. Most of the boys on Iwo were seventeen, eighteen, and nineteen years old.

The next guy is Rene' Gagnon from New Hampshire. Rene' kept a picture of his girlfriend in his helmet for protection. Young boys won the battle of Iwo Jima, not old men.

The third guy is Sergeant Mike Strank who was twenty four years old and hero to the younger kids. Mike sould say, "Listen to me and I'll get you home to your mothers."

The fourth guy is Ira Hayes, a Pima Indian from Arizona who walked off alive and later visited President Harry Truman in the White House. Hayes always felt guilty because out of 250 of his fellow marines, he and twenty-six others were the only survivors. Ira Hayes would die dead drunk ten years after the Iwo victory.

The next guy is Franklin Sousley from Hilltop, Kentucky, a fun-lovin' hillbilly boy who died at the age of nineteen. The telegram informing his mother was delivered from the nearby grocery store by a barefoot boy. Her nearest neighbor a quarter mile away could hear her screaming until the sunrise.

The next guy is John Bradley from Antigo, Wisconsin and lived until 1994. He would never submit to any interviews from any national TV network or newspaper. Bradley was a medic and watched over 200 boys die, writhing and screaming in pain. His philosophy, like so many others who returned safely was that the "real heroes of Iwo Jima never came back". Overall, over 7000 boys died on Iwo in the worst battle in Marine Corps history.

The monument isn't just a big old piece of metal with a flag flying on top but a testament to all the bravery and valor of all of our countrys military, who have served so proudly.

Image of the Marines after the flag was raised on Iwo Jima and my concept sketch of the raising.

COWBOYS, GUNS, AND HORSES

My mother had no professional skills or real training when my father died. And now, a widowed, single mother, she was left with the task of raising and supporting me, her only child. It was a daunting task but somehow, she managed.

At the time of my father's death, we were living in a two-bedroom apartment on Main Street. The apartment was located next door to a dry cleaner, RE Boone on Main Street in Burlington, North Carolina. The owner of the dry cleaner lived above the business and was divorced with two daughters. One of the daughters was my age and the other, a few years older. I enjoyed playing Hopscotch, a game today's children probably know nothing about, and I would play on the sidewalk in front of the apartment building. The daughters of the dry cleaner would talk to me from their lofty second floor perch and one day, when they saw me drawing the hopscotch marks on the sidewalk, they talked me into writing a word on the sidewalk. Instead of just saying the word, they spelled it out for me, it started with a "F" and ended with a "K". Being an innocent 7-year-old, I didn't understand why my mama got so mad at me when she saw my sidewalk art, but I promise you one thing for sure, she hurt a lot more than my feelings that day.

My mother kept food on our table by working in a textile mill. The textile trade was the backbone of the southern economy at the time, so jobs in that line of work were abundant in practically every small community in North Carolina. On her way to work she would leave me with friends, George and Bessie Smith. I came to love these great people as though they were my own family. George and Bessie had a daughter named Peggy who was ten years my senior and thought she was my boss. Even though there was no blood relation, I thought of Peggy as a sister, even calling her "Sis". And Peggy made me toe the line as any older sister should.

Shortly after the death of my father, Mom went to work for the dry cleaner, RE Boone, making $35.00 per week and moved us to a duplex on Washington Street. Washington Street wasn't far from our apartment, just a few blocks away. Mom didn't own a car, so we had to stay in a close proximity to the dry cleaners since she had to walk to work.

I grew up in a good neighborhood. Kids played outside unsupervised until after dark. It was a neighborhood where the doors were never locked. On warm nights, the screen door was the only door closed. And when my friends ran in and out at will for a glass of water or one of Mom's homemade cookies, you could hear that screen door slam all the way down the block. I was a normal boy. Rough housing, playing in the dirt, climbing trees, I did it all. I was an active kid, and active kids are rough on clothes. I remember going to school with patched jeans. In today's world, I would have been "styling".

George was a great lover of horses and bought and sold them as a sideline. He would buy the horses that needed the most attention, see to all their physical needs, fatten them up on lush green pasture and sell them for a nice profit.

From the moment George introduced me to horses, I was hooked. The only problem was, I lived in the city and everyone knows you can't have horses in the city. A vivid imagination was all I needed to bring my stick horse to life. I was always the good guy wearing the white hat and my buddies were always the villians. Our radio reception was iffy at best, so in order to listen to the Lone Ranger, we had a wire attached to the radio that went out the window and attached to a pole as a makeshift antenna. This wire was only a few feet off the ground and in the heat of the moment, running as fast as my stick horse would take me, trying to escape from the bad guys, I completely forgot about the antenna Mom had put up. I hit that wire at full speed. It caught me squarely under my lip just above my chin. Had it been any lower, I probably would have been decapitated. It would have been an awful way for the Good Guy to go out. God watches over children and fools.

I was left with a scar for a few years that finally disappeared.

I was only interested in riding stick horses and shooting outlaws, so I'm sure my mother probably figured I had an uncertain destiny. Things were so simple then. There were no gray areas; it was just black and white.

9

(Top Left to Right) Gene with Mom, with Dad
(Bottom Left to Right) Gene with his surrogate Family, and with Friends

THE BIG GUN

We moved to Anthony Street when I was seven or eight. Anthony Street is just off Webb Avenue, the main artery between Graham and Burlington. There was an intersection everyone knew as the "Big Gun" because a huge pre-WWII Navy cannon sat square in the middle of the road, a functional cannon at that. Legend has it, someone loaded the cannon one night and fired it toward Graham. After that night, city officials plugged it up.

Jack Howerton ran the Modern Shoe Shop at the "Big Gun" intersection along with his dad Charlie. Jack was a very talented man that made wallets and other things out of leather. For Christmas that year, Mom had Jack make me a leather two gun set of holsters with my name engraved on it. She added a matching pair of pearl handled, engraved Texan Junior cap pistols and a generous supply of caps. Around the same time, I got the nicest set of spurs. I killed many a bad hombre with those guns and had the fastest stick horse around when I had those spurs on. I was the envy of the entire neighborhood. Those pistols and holsters still hang in my office some seventy years later and when I can find caps, those guns still shoot just like they did when I was seven or eight.

The Big Gun up Close and at Intersection

Charlie, Jack Howerton's daddy, developed polio, and in that era, it was very debilitating. Polio would paralyze muscles in the chest making it impossible for a person to breathe. The person would have to lay on a metal bed inside the "Iron Lung" and let the machine breathe for them until they were well enough to breathe on their own. I remember Charlie lost the use of his legs and had to resort to using crutches. Jack, wanting his dad to be able to get around on his own, engineered a solution for Charlie's pickup where the gas and brakes were on the steering column, allowing Charlie to continue driving. These devices are readily available today, but imagine the conversation this stirred up around the woodstove in the 1950's. At 12, I went to work as a shoe shine boy for the barber shop next door to Jack's shoe shop making $0.25 and hour as well as a good friend in Jack.

Years later at a reunion for the guys from the "Big Gun", Jack told me he remembered making the holsters. I looked at him with a grin and said, "Well go ahead Jack, make my day".

I WANNA BE A COWBOY

George Smith owned a spotted mare that was gentle and an exceptional kids' horse. It was a beautiful sunny morning at about 10am when George coaxed me on her. Not that it took much more coaxing than a "Hey, do you want to ride?" to get me on her. Being on that horse was like being on the front of that Indian motorcycle with my father. I wore that mare out and I'm sure she was terribly relieved when George was finally able to get me off her around 6 pm. This began my love affair with horses and deepened my subconscious desire to be a cowboy.

Spending time with George and Bessie also meant I got to spend a lot of time around George's horses. And horses became my whole world. I craved going to Siler City, North Carolina to the horse sales with George and would marvel at the sound of the auctioneer's chant. Anticipation would build until he would bring down the gavel and shout "SOLD" and call out the number of the winning buyer.

Siler City was also the home of a celebrity. Mayberry's own Frances Bavier, "Miss Bee" from the "Andy Griffith Show" finished out her days in this sleepy southern town. When asked why she didn't return to her home state of New York, she said "I fell in love with North Carolina, all the pretty roads and the trees".

Going to the sale on Fridays with George, meant that I would get to eat some of the freshest hamburgers and best French fries in the state of North Carolina. Looking back, maybe they were so good because of where we were. Our trip home always meant a bag of of boiled peanuts to share on the way. Going to the sale was an all-day event, and we usually didn't arrive back home until 10:00 or 11:00pm. Saturday morning, I would jump up and hustle down to George and Bessie's for a huge home cooked breakfast and to check out the horse we had brought home the night before. Sometimes, the horse acted so different, I wasn't sure if it was the same horse George had bid on and bought. In those days there was a lot of doping going on and you may very well end up with a mustang on your hands. George was the original "Horse Wisperer" because after a few weeks or months went by when he was ready to sell the horse, it was always a different animal. George was great at buying what some would call a sack of bones. He would worm it and fatten it up. Its coat would glisten, and it would become the animal God created. It was a blessed animal that he purchased, and you could see it when the time came to take it back to the sale.

George with his Granddaughter

WHAT IS A COWBOY?

Someone once asked me what is a cowboy, and this was my reply. Son, a cowboy is a state of mind engulfed in honorable actions. He is a man of steel and velvet. He is putty in the hands of a small child and a true lady. He is a rock when circumstances require, not afraid to rise to the occasion. He is self assured enough to tip his hat to a lady, offer her his seat, open a door for her or help seat her at a table.

He shows respect to our flag and our country, crossing his heart with his hat at a rodeo, funeral procession, parade or any event where old glory is flown. He will bend his knee to help a small child or an elderly person and stands ever ready to lend a neighbor a helping hand. When tragedy befalls him, he will cowboy up and bear the brunt of it because to him that is the character of his breed. He has an inborn love of animals, especially horses.

He gives respect to those that deserve it and expects the same from them. He doesn't wear his religion on his sleeve but knows his strength is rooted in his maker. A cowboy is at home wherever he is because he's comfortable in his own skin. He needs no one in particular and yet he needs everybody. He can be your best friend or your worst enemy.

In short, I guess a cowboy is all that's good and right in this country and most true americans have a little bit of cowboy in them. A cowboy,– son–is not what he does it's who he is.

COMMON SENSE AIN'T COMMON ANYMORE

Or Rules A Cowboy Should Live By

Why worry about something that's never going to happen.
Live your life as though it were a sermon.
Make your fences strong enough to withstand a hurricane.
Check behind you occasionally to make sure the herd's still there.
How high you bounce is more important than how hard you fall.
A goat will always stand out in a flock of sheep.
Always go around the stump when plowing.
If you really want someone to comprehend, whisper, don't yell.
Meanness is acquired, ugliness is built in.
Be nice to your enemies, it always confuses them.
A plow's no good if you don't have a mule.
If it looks meaner than you, it's best to stay away from it.
When walking through life, stay away from the mudholes.
You can choose your friends, but you can't choose your relatives.
People will judge you as smart if you keep your mouth closed.
If a bobcat ain't bothering you, leave it alone.
If it's raining, you're too late with the rain dance.
Eating crow is a lot easier when it's warm.
Don't dig the hole any deeper than it already is.
The man in the mirror is sometimes your worst enemy.
When cows get stupid, they run while humans cover their eyes.
You might want to consider removing your spurs before squatting.
Courage is being scared to death, but slapping on the saddle anyway.

Common sense and wisdom are the best of friends, don't you think.

THE RUNNING MAN

While growing up on Main Street in the apartment next to RE Boone Cleaners we had a mailman that became quite the celebrity back in the early 40's. I didn't fully realize how big a celebrity he became until I was grown. Paul James Simpson brought the mail along with an occasional stick of gum or piece of candy to the kids in the neighborhood. He was more aptly known as Hardrock Simpson who began running as a Burlington High School track star in the 1920's.

What we weren't cognizant of as kids was the fact that he had outraced a horse from Burlington to Morehead City, a distance of over a hundred miles and worthy of being in Ripley's Believe It or Not. In 1927, according to Hardrocks own accounts, he raced a horse named Major in a race being held to promote Burlington and allow Hardrock to raise money so that he could take part in a cross-country foot race. Hardrock would end up running coast to coast twice in his lifetime. As our mailman, his daily procedure went something like this: deliver the mail on his 12-mile route on foot, lift weights and then run ten miles for his training program.

At 9 am September 1st, 1927, Hardrock, age 22 and the horse Major, ridden by Owen Faucette took off in race to Morehead City. Crowds lined both sides of Highway 70 to watch the spectacle. Surprisingly, when Hardrock was eating lunch in Durham, the horse was still 20 miles behind in Hillsborough.

In the state capital of Raleigh, some folks weren't aware of the race. They saw Hardrock running up the street and gave pursuit thinking he was an escapee from Dorothea Dix Mental Institution, there in the city. That chase, of course, was an exercise in futility.

Hardrock ended the first day at a hotel in Raleigh, where he spent the night. Unbeknownst to Hardrock, at 3am the next morning, Faucette jumped on Major and left, giving the horse a sizeable three-hour lead. The outside temperature was 102 degrees and people along the sides of the road were calling Hardrock a fool and urging him to quit. But Hardrock, with his usual crooked teeth grin blissfully ignored the crowd. He caught up with Major outside of Goldsboro. It was an even sprint through the town limits. About three miles from downtown, the horse collapsed and could not be revived. Hardrock continued his run to the next town of Kinston where he was informed that he had won the race.

On his 50th birthday, Hardrock started running a mile for each year of his life. He continued that tradition into his late 60's. He died in July 1978 at the age of 73. He left a legacy no one has matched. The thing I remember most about our mailman, the runningest man in Alamance County history was his infectious smile and the occasional Tootsie Roll he would dole out to the kids, me included.

Photo credit of Burlington Times News, written by Jim Wicker, January 7,1992

WHOA BESS!

In addition to my "adopted" family George and Bessie, my mother had two siblings, Grace and Taylor. The three siblings, all had one child each, Grace had a daughter, Diana and Taylor a son, Jimmy. Since we were the only children of the respective families, we were very close. In today's terms, when opportunity provided, we could be found "hanging out".

Aunt Grace's husband was Zollie and like most men, Zollie enjoyed meal time. In those days, the biscuits were made fresh and the meals were a time where the whole family was seated together to share their food. The blessing would be said, and the fixin's, would be passed around the table from person to person. Diana about five, watched as the biscuits were passed around finally ending up at her father, Zollie. In the innocence of a five-year-old, Diana exclaimed loudly "Watch him, watch him, watch him take two". You will be happy to hear that Diana survived the incident. She turned out to be an extraordinary individual whom I care for greatly. She later married Jerry Cummings, a Lieutenant Colonel in the Marines and they have two sons Kyle, a Federal Air Marshal and Kelly, a North Carolina SBI agent.

Mom's brother Taylor was a school board member and a very active member of his community in Bolivia, North Carolina, where he also had a tobacco farm.

I was the man of the house from an early age so as soon as I was old enough, 11 or 12, I took a job with a local newspaper as a delivery boy. I made enough money to help Mom with the expenses and have some spending money. Looking back, I'm sure those were tough times. But I really don't remember the hard times that way. I just remember enjoying life.

Enjoying life while working hard continued into my High School years. Summer time meant tobacco season and working on Taylor's farm.

Uncle Taylor loved having me around for the free "slave" labor. In those days, the blacks and whites coexisted without friction and as I worked in the tobacco field, I worked hand in hand with some very knowledgeable blacks who knew the tobacco business well. Believe me when I say, tobacco farming is the hardest, nastiest work I have ever done, in my entire life. When the tobacco was "in", we worked from sunrise to sunset. Our only break was a very short lunch. For me, the short lunch break usually included a quick nap and a sandwich. Man, a union man would have hated the hours and working conditions. But I grabbed a nap to restore enough energy to get back in the fields and finish out the day cropping tobacco. The tobacco was collected in a homemade two by six-foot sled framed with burlap siding and a wooden bottom drawn by a mule. Uncle Taylor had a mule, Bess. Bess was in harness, but when she was in the rows, the reins usually just hung around her neck. She had heard her two commands "get up" and "whoa" so many times, she was well informed on her duties. After a grueling day in the tobacco field, the highlight of mine and Jimmy's day was to ride Bess back to the barn in the afternoon.

I remember one time Uncle Tayor told Bess to "get up", to which she fully complied. But once she "got up", she didn't stop. She just kept going, ignoring Uncle Taylor yelling "whoa". Taylor, not lacking in colorful words hollered in a loud voice "I said whoa, you son of a bitch". Well I guess Bess didn't appreciate the slander on her familys name, because not only did she not whoa, she took off running. Did I forget to mention she was attached to the sled at the time? What Taylor did when he caught her would be fodder for any SPCA (Society for Prevention of Cruelty to Animals) lawyer today. Let's just suffice to say it was not a pretty sight. Bess never pulled that stunt again.

Jimmy and I had a wonderful childhood on the farm. Uncle Taylor owned a 1937 Chevy truck with a 4-speed shift in the floor. Jimmy and I would drop the tailgate and jump on, dragging our feet in the sand while Uncle Taylor "cruised" down the sandy road. Once we hit the hard surface road, we'd pull our feet up and continue down the road. God watches over fools and children.

Everyday during the summer, when we were through working for the day, we would go down the road to the country store for an RC Cola and a MoonPie. That was our big reward for a hard day's work, and we looked forward to it everyday. I can honestly say, I have worked for peanuts.

The cousins, Jerry and Diana, Gene and Jimmy, Uncle Taylor

The summers weren't all work and on days when we weren't working, Jimmy and I had fun. We got to hang out and go to dances and ogle over the local girls.

At the end of a long and tiring week of putting up and curing tobacco in the barns, it was time to head to the auction. We would load that old Chevy to the hilt and drive it to the tobacco auction in Whiteville. Whiteville was forty miles away and Jimmy and I were so excited because we got to ride on top of all that tobacco the whole way. The tobacco was piled higher than the cab of the truck. So Jimmy and I had the best view in the house.

That Chevy was loaded down with cured tobacco hanging over the sides and piled a good foot above the cab. The weight was so heavy the fender wells almost scraped the tires, the rear bumper only inches from dragging the road. And perched on top of that pile, sat me and Jimmy. The front end was so elevated from the weight of the tobacco my Uncle had to take it slow; otherwise we would have been weaving all over the road. Can you envision such a scenario? It looked like the opening scene of The Beverly Hillbillies with Old Lizzie loaded down with furniture and critters and Jethro and Elllie May sitting on top, smiling from ear to ear. I can see a patrolmans face pulling up on that today. I mean really, two teenagers riding on top of a 10 foot pile of tobacco in a moving vehicle. Not on your life. Of course, back then everywhere Taylor went in that truck, Jimmy and I were riding in the back of it. And boy, did we love it! Seriously, we obviously made it out alive, or I would not be here to write this saga.

Once we got to the warehouse, we had to unload all this tonnage and stack it on pallets. Tobacco is stacked in what they refer to as grades. Most of the time, because of our slow driver, brought on by hauling two boys on a ton of tobacco, we wouldn't get to the auction until late in the evening. By the time we unloaded and got a bite to eat we were exhausted and there were no silk sheets for us. We slept on the pallets of tobacco we rode in on! And except for the smell; they were amazingly comfortable. It was like sleeping on down stuffing.

It was mesmerizing following the auctioneer down the aisles and listening to his chant. He was so rapid in his speech I had no idea what he was saying but I guess the buyers knew. The only thing I understood was "sold to American". When I heard those words, I knew the American Tobacco Company had bought that lot. I believe tobacco sold for about $0.70 per lb.

I didn't know it at the time, but my circle would become smaller as one of my Theta Chi fraternity brothers, Kirby Branch's daddy was one of the auctioneers. Mr. Branch was nationally known and pictured in a Lucky Strike ad on the back cover of Life magazine. He was a nice gentleman and always treated me well during my college years when I would stay with Kirby's family at their home in Greenville, North Carolina.

I gained a great deal of respect for the American farmer from those days of growing up and working on Uncle Taylor's farm. While I wasn't overly excited about the work, I loved the experience and the strength of character it instilled in me. As my dear mama used to say "Son, don't ever get above your raising". Amazing how much wiser the older folks are when you are young and how much wiser you become as you age.

GRANDDADDY

In 1956, the road to Uncle Taylor's farm was long and sandy with the farm about a mile off the main highway. Today, the road is paved, and it's been named Taylor Albright Road, after Uncle Taylor.

On that long, sandy road in my Uncle Taylor's 1937 Chevy truck, Uncle Taylors wife, Marie, taught me to drive. It was a 4-speed in the floor when we started, but much to her chagrin, I may have reduced it to a three speed after constantly grinding the gears.

Mom, Grace, and Taylor's father was Rufus Eugene Albright. Rufus Albright was lovingly called Granddaddy and Granddaddy loved to fish. Fishing is a sport I have never been able to acquire a taste for. I could never understand being happy about sitting for hours on end waiting for some tiny bit of activity to occur. But Granddaddy would visit Uncle Taylor's farm several times while I was there during the summer so he could fish.

Granddaddy making ice cream, Grandaddy and buddies fishing

In those days there were no indoor bathrooms. You had only outdoor privies, known as outhouses, and if the privy was occupied, you grabbed a corn shuck or a Sears Roebuck catalog (yes kids, it was Roebuck once) or anything else that may handle the job for Charmin toilet paper and head for the woods.

On an evening during one of these trips, Granddaddy headed for the woods across the road from the house. Jimmy and I had walked to the store for our RC Cola and MoonPie and playing around like boys will, we were running late coming back. Darkness was settling in, and it was eerily quiet, the animals, critters and bugs settled down for the night. The only sound to be heard was me and Jimmy rough housing and carrying on. We were thirty yards from the house when all of a sudden, we heard a noise from the woods. The brush was moving, and sounds were coming out of there like a bobcat. We took off running for the house, tripping over our feet. To this day, I can't tell you whether Jimmy or I opened that screen door first. The one thing I do know for sure is I will never forget the sound of Granddaddy's laughter as he came through that same screen door seconds after we did, after his visit to the woods.

THE CUSTOMS THAT SURVIVED

The next time you are washing your hands and complain because the temperature isn't just right, remember this: In the 1500's most people got married in June because they took their yearly bath in May. By June the bride was starting to smell a little and they carried a bouquet of flowers to hide the body odor. Hence; the custom today of carrying a bouquet of flowers when getting married.

Baths consisted of a huge tub filled with hot water. The man of the house was privileged to bathe first, then the sons and other men. Finally, the women and children. Last of all the babies. By then the water was so dirty you could lose someone in it. Hence; the saying 'don't throw the baby out with the bathwater.

Houses had thatched roofs (thick straw piled high) with no wood underneath. It was the only place for animals to get warm, so all the cats and other small animals (mice, bugs, etc.) lived in the roof. When it rained, the roof became slippery and sometimes the animals would fall off. Hence; the saying 'its raining cats and dogs'.

There was nothing to stop things from falling into the house, which posed a real problem in the bedroom where droppings and bugs could mess up your nice clean bed. Hence a bed with big posts with a sheet hung over the top. The advent of the canopy bed.

The floor was dirt which is where "dirt poor" came from since only the wealthy had slate floors. In the winter the floors would get slippery when wet, so they spread thresh (straw) on the floor to keep their footing. As winter wore on they added more thresh until, when you opened the door, the thresh would slip outside. A piece of wood was put in the entrance way. Hence; a thresh hold.

The wives cooked in a big kettle pot over an open fire and every day that they lit the fire they would add new ingredients to the pot. It was mostly vegetables. They would leave the leftovers to get cold overnight and then start over the next day. Sometimes food had been in the pot quite a while. Hence; the rhyme "peas porridge hot, peas porridge cold, peas porridge in the pot, nine days old".

When visitors came over, people would hang up their bacon, since in those days it was a sign of wealth that a man could "bring home the bacon". They would cut off a little to share with guests and would all sit around and 'chew the fat". Those with money had plates made of pewter and food with acid content caused some of the lead to leach onto the food causing lead poisoning death. This mostly happened with tomatoes, so for the next four hundred years or so, tomatoes were consdiered poisonous.

Bread was divided according to status. Workers got the burnt bottom of the loaf. The family got the middle and guests got the top, or the "upper crust". Lead cups were used to drink ale or whiskey and sometimes the combination would knock the imbibers out for a couple days. Someone walking down the road would see them lying there and take them for dead and prepare them for burial. They were laid out on the kitchen table for a couple days while the family would gather around eating and drinking and waiting to see if they would wake up. Hence; the custom "holding a wake".

Since England is a small country, local folks started running out of places to bury people. They would dig up coffins and take the bones to a bone-house and reuse the grave. When reopening these coffins, one out of twenty-five had scratch marks on the inside and they realized they had been burying people alive. From then on, they would tie a string around the wrist of the body feeding it through the coffin, up through the ground and tie it to a bell. Someone would sit in the graveyard all night (the graveyard shift) to listen for the bell. Thus, "someone could be saved by the bell" or was considered "a dead ringer".

Just thought these were some interesting facts well worth sharing. Just remember inside every older person is a younger person wondering "what the heck happened". Nobody can ever claim that history is dull, only the presentation of it.

MY DREAMS CAME TRUE FOR $0.35

The small town of Graham is the county seat of Alamance County. In the 1940's, Graham was home to two theatres, the Alco and the Graham Theatre. The Alco has been closed for decades, but the Graham Theatre is still going strong at the ripe old age of 100. Recreational entertainment of the video nature was practically non-existent in those days so the theatre's supplied a wonderful treat for kids and adults alike.

The Alco played mostly westerns and since all young boys wanted to be cowboys, the Alco was the most popular. It was $0.25 admission and $0.10 for popcorn and a drink. In those days, the western stars would make personal appearances on stage at these Matinees. They would promote their movies by showing up at the theatre either before the movie started or after it ended. And that was a young cowboy's dream world.

His name was actually Alred LaRue, but as many actors; he changed it to a more suitable screen name, Lash LaRue. He came in and brought his horse on stage. Lash LaRue wore all black with a pearl handle pistol on his right side and his whip on his left. The man was amazing and awed the audience with his feats. He used his whip to flick a cigarette out of the mouth of a willing audience member. He extinguished a flame from a candle and then proceeded to take the top off of a watermelon. He never touched anything other than his intended target. There were no stunt doubles, cuts or do-overs folks, this was live and it was the real thing. Lash LaRue's skills were so well known, he went on to teach Harrison Ford how to use a bullwhip for the Indiana Jones movies.

Long before he became King of the Cowboys, Roy Rogers, whose real name was Leonard Sly, came to Graham to promote his movie and brought his horse, Trigger. Trigger was a Tennessee Walking Horse and Roy trained him to obey seventy-six verbal commands.

On Saturday's, George and I would head to the Alco. It was an exciting time when Hollywod came to our small town and George enjoyed it as much as I did. We tried to make it a weekly excursion and my Saturdays at the Alco with George was the closet thing to heaven I could imagine. It helped get me through the difficult period of losing my father at such a young age. Often, we would stay and watch it a second time, I always looked forward to my Saturdays with George.

Main Street Graham and the Alco, Gene with
first car, Mom leaning on first car

Burlington is the largest city in the county of Alamance and is only a few miles away from Graham. Burlington had four theatres in the 1940's, The State, The Alamance, The Paramount and The Town. All are gone now except the Paramount. It has been retained as a Gallery Players Live Event Theatre. My cousin, Diana, has appeared in several plays at the Paramount.

While in high school, I worked at The State running the concessions. After everyone was seated, there was nothing really left for me to do so I would stand at the back of the theatre and watch the movie. This meant I watched each movie about three times a day for about four or five days. By the time the movie left the theatre, I had the dialogue memorized.

As I look back to my time working at the theatre, I suppose it was inevitable that I end up in the entertainment field after being exposed to so many movies growing up. I held numerous jobs over the years and did not shy away from hard work. And though I held several jobs, I had only two dominant occupations, sales and journalism. I loved both passionately.

The job at the theatre provided me with enough income to buy my first car. It was a 1941 Chevy Sedan but for me, it may have very well been a Rolls Royce. At this time, Mom was still working at the dry cleaners and money was tight. My options were buy my own car or keep walking. $600.00 bought me freedom to be more independent. When you are making $0.75 cents an hour, $600.00 is a fortune.

After I purchased my first car, I was hooked and never seemed totally satisfied with any one car. I was always on the lookout for a faster, more stylish one. It seemed like the bulk of the money I made was spent on buying or refurbishing a different car. I was like most teenage boys of the day and thought there were some really classics coming out of Detroit. Now you can't tell the difference between one from another without a magnifying glass.

I got interested in drag racing back when world-famous local boys Ronnie Sox and Richard Petty were making a name for themselves. With the help of a local man, Noel Gusler (an expert in building six-cylinder engines), I rebuilt the six cylinders on a 1947 Chevy coupe. We devised a three-line carburetor system that would open all three carburetors at the same time, beefed up the oil pump and shaved the heads to give it greater combustion. That car would burn the rubber off the rear tires. I never faced

Richard Petty, but I did have an occasion to face Ronnie Sox. It was the original tortoise and the hare story. I was the tortoise.

In high school, I owned a 1950 Oldsmobile Rocket 88. It was one of the fastest cars on the road back then. It would raise up in the rear end when you accelerated. Ronnie and I attended the same high school, so one day, I very foolishly challenged him to a race. He was driving a Mercury Comet with three on the column and he was never one to turn down a challenge. I don't have to tell you who won.

Ronnie Sox at his race car

Ronnie was the best I ever encountered at speed shifting. He was so fast; you could barely see his hands move. Ronnie passed away several years ago, but not until he became world famous with the Sox and Martin team. The team traveled all over the world drag racing. Most of the time, Ronnie would win.His brother David, who worked at the local Chevrolet dealership, has sold me several trucks over the years.

I finally got out of racing when I realized I didn't have enough funds to pursue that hobby and was only making Sumners Automotive richer. It was one of lifes great experiences. Like most men, I loved the sports cars. I especially loved the early Corvettes. Over the years, I have owned a 1958, 1962, 1964 1972 and a 1980, all of which I wish I had retained. The 1964 had four in the floor with a 454 big block. It would reach about 75 miles per hour in a quarter mile. It was so powerful it would pin you against the seat on take off. Amazing how I survived that car.

JUDY

During my adolescence, I attended several different elementary schools, most of which no longer exist due to consolidation of the school system. I remember schools such as Fisher Street, Maple Avenue and Pine Top. I went to Broad Street Junior High before entering the "new" Walter M. Williams High School. It was built in 1951 and named after a local industrialist. It was the most modern high school in the state. My class was the first to graduate the full four-year completion of the new school. During my school years, I enjoyed the arts and science classes. English was far from my favorite subject. However, I am amazed at how much I have retained over the years. My English teacher would be proud considering the career path I would later follow.

Not unlike most teens of the day I enjoyed myself. I was in the scouts early on, joined the order of the DeMolay, a subsidiary group of the Masons, and played football with the Williams Bulldogs. My football career was short and sweet. I took one too many bad hits and messed up my knee which still troubles me to this day when the weather is humid. Girls were always on a young man's mind and I was no exception. I met my wife, Judy while spending time at my Aunt Grace's house. Judy lived in Graham, a few houses down from Aunt Grace on Westover Street. I first saw her when I was still in elementary school and a bunch of the neighborhood boys and girls would get together and play hide and seek. One of the kid's dad had rigged a tall swing from a huge oak tree. Judy was on the swing and somebody, for all I know it could have been me, pushed her too high. She fell from the swing and broke her arm.

Gene with School Friends, Gene and Judy Senior Year

I had not given up my cowboy ways. I sawed wooden pistols with an eight-inch barrel out of plywood. Then I fastened a clothespin to the heel of the gun with nails and wrapped it tightly with circular pieces cut from an inner tube. I cut an oval circle and tied a knot in the center making it into a figure eight. This was my ammo and when I stretched it across the length of that eight-inch barrel and let it go, it had quite a wallop, at close range it could raise a blister.

I used to enjoy chasing the girls and shooting at them with my wooden pistols. They got to where they didn't want to play with me and run away saying "Here comes that mean Gene Hunter". For the life of me I couldn't understand why. I didn't really care about the other girls. I just wanted to see Judy run, she had the prettiest legs. I guess the others didn't really understand my motives. I think that's when I first fell in love with her, way back then.

Judy went on to become a head cheerleader at Graham High. She was a member of the National Honor Society and voted best personality in her class as well as most liked and valedictorian her senior year. She was on the debate team. It wasn't until after we were married for forty years, I came to realize just how well she had honed that skill. She always won the debates even if I never fully realized it until it was all over.

During our years in school, Judy and I dated off and on. We even went steady a couple of times, but the timing wasn't right and when High School was over, she went to Women's College in Greensboro, now UNC-G, and I went to East Carolina University. Life separated us. I would hear from her often and see her from time to time, but I was busy with my life and she was busy with hers.

PHI GAMMA PI

When I began at East Carolina it was known as East Carolina College (ECC). In later years, thanks to the efforts of state senator and former State Attorney General Robert Morgan, it became East Carolina University.

When I enrolled in college, I was looking forward to life in the dormitory. I was assigned to Slay Dormitory Annex, a small two-bedroom arrangement with a kitchen, bath and living room. At first, I was disappointed, but at the same time got along great with the other three roommates. No curfew, no lights out, no bed check. We had our independence and made a pact to respect each others privacy. It worked out well.

And, with everything I was involved in, I was rarely there. One of my roommates, Jesse Watts was the greatest guy you ever wanted to meet. He had a deformity in one arm, but his personality was such that you never even noticed his arm. He was the hardest working student I knew and fully realized why he was there. His routine was the same every day: classes, then work at a local hot dog stand until eight, and back to the room to study until midnight. I have no doubt he finished his degree and probably joined a Harvard Law Firm. His work ethic was never upset the entire time I roomed with him. I wish some of Jesse's work ethic had rubbed off on me. I was far too busy learning life's real lessons and I'm not sure when I found time to study, but I maintained an acceptable grade.

The school was busting at the seams in the fall of 1957. By reputation, it was, and still is, a party school. And people came from all over to join the party. The social functions were endless, and I felt right at home. About mid-year of my freshman year I realized there were no men's social fraternities on campus. Although, I have never thought of myself as a leader, I do tend to jump in with ideas. So, I started contacting fellow classmates.

Nearly 60 years ago, late one evening, I met up with Phillip Haynes and Hughes Giles on the steps of Shea Dorm. We decided to form a fraternity and and to name it Phi Gamma Pi and I volunteered to write the constitution. Once that was done, we rounded up seventeen other guys and formed a charter to submit to the school student body. When we held elections, I was voted the first President of Phi Gamma Pi. Johnny Ferguson was voted as my Vice President.

Being a social fraternity, we decided to get sociable. After the elections, we all went out and got well wasted. I was pretty out of it and on the way back to my dorm room I decided I needed to relieve myself, making like a boy dog on one of the well-lit manicured campus trees. As I saw it, I was just trying to help mother nature. As fate would have it, a campus policeman showed up about that time and turned my name in to the Warden. We had a Dean of Men, Tucker, who we all referred to lovingly, as the Warden. Oh, what a crisis. The next day I appeared before Dean Tucker. I must have smoothed my way out of it because he told me he would let me off under one condition. The condition was that I sit down and write my mother and explain to her what had happened. All of it! Ouch! It was that or suspension. It was honestly the toughest decision of my life. I rarely drank and Mom had no idea about the few times I had. Reluctantly, I agreed and wrote the heartbreaking letter.

Believe it or not, that wasn't the worst part. The new fraternities charter was to be presented by the Presidents of the fraternities to the SGA (student government association) the next day. Dean Tucker was advisor to the SGA, so you can understand our problem. In a parliamentary move, we called an emergency meeting of the fraternity, and voted Johnny in as temporary president. This way he could present the charter instead of me. After the charter was approved the group reversed our roles and Phi Gamma Pi was legal.

One of the first pledges in the new fraternity was a young man named Bill Wallace. He was a bright student and a hard worker. Bill and another pledge Seaton Poe Fairless Jr. decided to take a trip to my hometown in Alamance County. They visited the jail and asked if they could spend the night in one of the cells. Yes, you read that correctly, it was voluntary. While in the area, Bill was to look up Judy and get her signature on his pledge paddle. Well, Bill decided to take it a step further and he and

Seaton talked Judy and my cousin Diana into donning a bathing suit and walking down Main Street in Burlington. Now this was on a busy Saturday afternoon but Bill told the girls they wouldn't be able to pledge if they didn't complete the assignment. Remember, this was the fifties, folks, so the bathing suits were one piece. Fortunately, it wasn't quite as bad as it sounds. They donned the bathing suits, walked out on the street about thirty feet for the photographer and then dashed back inside the store. The picture, ended up in the newspaper and Judy's daddy was not at all happy about it. It was a few months before I felt it was safe to come back home. Leave it to Bill.

Later in life, Bill became upper management of Hickey Freemans Menswear in New York City, clothiers for many of our nation's Presidents.

One of my closest brothers in the fraternity was Kirby Branch, whose father was the auctioneer at the tobacco auction. We went to the beach a lot in those days and held our first pledge class initiation on one of them. It was a cold, rainy night in January or February. We made the pledges strip to the buff, which was, in and of itself, inhumane. Then we blindfolded them, rubbed syrup and catsup on their head, made them swallow a raw oyster and told them it was a fish eye. After a few beers some of them didn't get it down. The only way to clean up was a dip in the ocean. Thinking back, I'm surprised they didn't get pneumonia. I guess the alcohol kept them warm. Naturally, afterwards we provided warm blankets and a campfire and welcomed them as new brothers.

I owned a black and white 1956 Chevy convertible. Oh, how I wish I still owned that one. After classes, I would grab Kirby, another brother, along with a case of beer and a girl and drive about thirty miles to the beach. I would turn up my Zenith AM transistor radio, which I still own today, and we would dance on the beach. Now that was the original shagging. After sunset we would build a fire, talk, and dance until late in the night. Sometimes we even slept on the beach and woke to watch the sunrise.

The fraternity later became affiliated with Theta Chi and is now a national fraternity. Recently they built a new half million-dollar fraternity house. Though I don't get back very often to "pirate country", I keep in touch with some of the brothers and know the fraternity is in good hands.

Kirby graduated from ECU in the ROTC program with a Second Lieutenant commission. He entered the Air Force and became a jet pilot. In many of our wide-ranging discussions throughout the years, I learned his final years before retirement were spent flying high ranking generals all over the world for important conferences. He would fly into Paris, spend two or three days-always on call and then fly them home. It's tough duty but somebody has to do it, right? He currently lives at his home place with his sweet wife Carol. It's the same horse farm where he grew up in Greenville and where I visited with his family so many years ago in school. Kirby is a very intelligent person with seemingly endless knowledge about anything you want to discuss. It amazes me sometimes how God packed so much smarts into one man.

At the same time, I was involved in the fraternity, I was still interested in radio. The campus had a small wattage station that barely went to the city limits of Greenville. But, hey! it was broadcasting. I applied for a job and was hired. It was a start in something I really loved. Early on, I realized how important it was in the business to get mileage behind the mike, and I wanted that.

Bill convincing the girls, Judy and Diana walking down Main Street

NURSES IN THE SHOWER

During my sophmore year, I met Charlie Briggs. He asked me to join the East Carolina Playhouse. Being behind a mike on the radio was one thing, but a live audience? Well, it's all entertainment I guess. Now what I'm going to say, you may find hard to believe given my track record. Performing in front of people has always been a terrifying experience for me. But like a moth drawn to a flame, I couldn't stay away. So, I joined the playhouse.

Our first production was also Charlie's first attempt at directing. It was *Mr. Roberts*. *Mr. Roberts* is a Broadway play and movie starring Henry Fonda as Mr. Roberts and Jack Lemmon as Ensign Pulver. My role in the play was a seaman named Stefanowski. My most memorable line was when the crew members were using binoculars to scope out the nurse's quarters. When my turn came for the binoculars, I looked out over the audience supposedly staring at the nurse's quarters and exclaimed in a stutter "Look she's taking a sh--sh--shower". That one line brought down the house.

Cast of Mr. Roberts

Ben Waters was another seamen in the play. He and I pulled off an authentic looking fight scene. I would cross paths with Ben later in life as he would be my news director at WGHP-TV in High Point and would eventually land at WBT-TV in Charlotte.

The cast and crew of *Mr. Roberts* was widely acclaimed under Charlie's direction. The play was supposed to run for five nights but was so successful the townspeople requested a holdover for another week. He was a talented director. I remember sitting down at a booth in the student union. He would be nearby writing his next play. He kept telling me he was going to Hollywood and urging me to come with him. I knew he was good, but I wasn't ready for Hollywood. Well he did it…. He left school the next semester and headed to Tinsel Town. Over the next eighteen years, he appeared in over 30 movies. Mostly bit parts. He was Muley in *Merrills Marauders* with Jeff Chandler, one of the hecklers in *Home from the Hill* with Robert Mitchum and George Hamilton and the goon in *The Absent-Minded Professor* with Fred MacMurray and numerous others. He was never cast in a large role, but he was steadily working. He returned to the Carolinas and opened The Tarheelian Playhouse, a live theatre outside of

Raleigh, but unfortunately, it flopped. In hindsight, maybe I should have gone to Hollywood, because I always considered myself a better actor than Charlie. I guess we'll never know.

That year, I met a girl named Marvis. She bowled me over with her looks. She reminded me of Donna Douglas as Ellie May Clampett. But unlike Ellie May, she had the brains to go along with the looks. She could twirl flaming batons as an act and had never met a stranger. We were both members of the playhouse and shared a love for acting. After dating for several months, I thought she was the one. I proposed and she accepted.

SECOND CHANCES

Judy's daddy was JV Meacham. When I first met him, he was working in a textile mill by day and painting cars at night in his garage. In between all that, he was taking a correspondence course in electronics, longing for the day when he could quit the mill. By the time Judy went to college, her Daddy had left textiles and opened his own business repairing radios and televisions in Graham. At the end of her sophmore year, Judy's father had a heart attack. Judy felt that it would be too much of a burden on him for her to continue college. So she quit and came home.

At the end of each school year, I came home for the summer. Graham is a small town where everyone knows everyone else. It didn't take long for me to hear about JV and that Judy was back home. It also didn't take long for me to visit to make sure the family was okay.

As soon as I saw Judy, I realized I had never stopped loving her. There was no way I could marry anyone else. I broke off my engagement with Marvis.

I started seeing Judy shortly after. She invited me to the Meacham family reunion in Rockingham, North Carolina. Rockingham was JV's homeplace and is located 60 miles south of Graham.

JV had recently bought a brand new 1958 Chevy Impala convertible. It was black with blue interior and a white top. He liked sporty cars too, probably why we hit it off so well. For some reason, Judy could not leave for the reunion with the rest of the family and since the family didn't want to be late, everyone rode with Judy's brother Barry, in his 1951 Ford and Judy and I followed a few hours later in her Daddy's Chevy. The car had a 396 three speed on the column with three two-barrel progressive carburetors. This car would do eighty in second gear. Trust me, I know.

We had the top down, Judy was driving, and we were cruising along at the speed limit, enjoying the music on the radio. It couldn't have been a more perfect day. About fifteen or twenty miles before we reached Rockingham, I convinced Judy to let me drive. I was chomping at the bit to get in the driver's seat, but it took some serious smooth talking until she finally relented. JV never found out about this or he would have blown a gasket and very likely have had a second heart attack.

I walked around the car, slid under the wheel, fastened my seat belt and got back on the highway. We were on a long, lonely, straight stretch of newly paved road on a Sunday morning. There were no cars in sight in either direction, I could feel the surge of power through the gas pedal and the moment was too tempting to pass up. So I wound it out, shifted to second and floored it. The car fishtailed, pinning Judy in the seat. I was up to eighty by the time I shifted to third and one hundred ten by the time I let off the gas. I still had a fourth of the pedal left. The car would have easily done one hundred and forty.

Judy was livid. She made me pull over and she drove the rest of the way. But I found out what was under the hood and being in the dog house for a few days was a fair price to pay. I guarantee no one ever drove that car that fast. God looks after kids and fools. Judy never told anybody; probably for fear her daddy wouldn't let her drive the car anymore. I asked JV, always addressed as Mr. Meacham, how fast he thought the car would go. His reply "I'll probably never know, I've never had it over 70." I just looked at Judy and grinned. She was having a hard time not laughing out loud.

On the trip back, JV and Eva was in the front and Judy and I were in the back. We were following Barry back home in his 1951 Ford. He had just installed glass pack mufflers that, because of the noise were illegal. Two miles from home, a North Carolina Highway patrolman pulled in behind Barry and flipped on his blue light, signaling Barry to pull over. JV pulled over as well. When the patrolman asked Barry to step out of the car, JV got out and walked toward the patrolman to see what was going on. When the patrolman saw JV, he rested his hand on his pistol and ordered him back in his car. The entire time this was happening, I could think of nothing more than how happy I was this patrolman wasn't behind me in Rockingham. They would have locked me up and thrown away the key.

Judy and I dated for six months and broke up again. I don't even remember why. She entered into a whirlwind courtship, became engaged and was married a few months later. My heart was broken. The thought of seeing Judy in town with another man was too much to handle. I had no desire to return to college and never did.

I enlisted in the air force six weeks later.

CHAPTER 2

LIFE IN THE AIR FORCE

Watch Tower at Ramey AFB

BARRACKS CHIEF

In 1959, my mother married my stepfather, George Vestal. The time was right to move forward with my life. I was going into the Armed Services.

Since my father had enlisted in the Marines, I also desperately wanted to join the Marines. I felt it was continuing a family tradition since we also had other "Jarheads" in the family; my cousin and two of my aunts and uncles, not to mention Judy's father, JV.

My mother was so distraught when I told her my plan, she wouldn't hear of it. I succumbed to her wishes and in the Fall of 1959, enlisted in the Air Force. The first stop on my military adventure was basic training at Lackland Air Force Base, San Antonio, Texas.

Little did Mom or I realize since I was going into security, I would be going through the same basic training as the Marines. But I loved it! I was six foot tall and had been lifting weights for the past year, so I was 180 pounds of muscle. The Drill Sergeant, a former Marine, interviewed the fifty or so men in our squad for Barracks Chief. The Barracks Chief would oversee the men in the squad when the sergeant was not there. The hard work of the past year paid off and I was chosen.

I guess every day was just another day at the office for the Drill Sergent. When 1700 rolled around, 5pm to you civilians, the Drill Sargeant gave me any instructions he deemed fitting and headed for the local bar. I was left in charge of those fifty rookies. Most evenings he wouldn't come back until 0300 or 0400 in the morning. As a rule, he could sleep until 0600. I would get the men up and supervise that everyone was showered and shaved, and the barracks squared away by 0500. Then, I would march them the quarter mile to and from the chow hall. When you have a crew of 50 to feed, it requires about an hour and a half. That put us getting back to the barracks about 0700, where we were met by a freshly starched, bright eyed, hung over Sergeant. I came to view him as somewhat of a superman, but realize he probably died of schlorsis of the liver at a fairly young age. He was a top sergeant though, and he knew his stuff.

I must have earned his respect early on because he seemed to have full confidence in me, which helped make my job with the men a lot easier. Most of the men understood and respected my position because from the onset, the Sergeant had made it perfectly clear to them that if I gave them an order it was as direct as if it came from him. But theres always one, isn't there?

My one was a smart guy of spanish descent who was always testing me. Last to shave, last to shower, never had his area squared away and in general just had a lack of self discipline.

In San Antonio, the temperature reaches one hundred degrees and above early in the day, so we were all assigned pith helmets, the kind Jungle Jim wears in the movies, to protect us from the sun. Well, Jose which we shall call him (since sixty years has eroded his name) was up to his usual antics. I had marched the squad back to the barracks and, as fate would have it, the sergeant had experienced an unusually rough night, so he left the morning inspection up to me. There were probably seventy-five to eighty barracks spaced about thirty yards apart with a concrete walk going down the middle. The squads would all form behind their respective barracks for inspection and the morning PT. I had formed our squad behind our barracks in extended formation and at attention for inspection. There were four rows with Jose being on the last row just about two feet from the barracks. He was doing what he usually did to me, looking around, taking a visual tour like he had never seen the place before. He finally got on my last nerve; not to mention he was making the squad look bad in front of the other squadrons. So, when I saw what he was doing I plowed through the ranks of four deep until I got to him. He was about my size. I grabbed him by the collar, slammed him against the barracks wall and threatened to mop up the ground with him if he didn't straighten up his act. His pith helmet shot off his head like a rocket and went flying out to the center walkway and landed at the feet of a Master Sergeant that happened to be passing by. Seeing what had just occurred he motioned for me to come over to him. My first thought was "Lord, I'm in deep trouble", except trouble wasn't exactly the word I thought. He walked me away, out of earshot of the squad, which I had just put at ease, and whispered in my ear, "Son, I don't care if you beat the hell out of him, just don't do it in public". I thanked the sergeant, picked up the helmet and handed it to Jose. Then I ordered him back in the ranks. From that day forward, Jose never gave me a minute's trouble. In fact, he turned out to be one fine airman. I guess he just needed somebody to get the message across that he could do better.

Little did I know that all the knowledge and experience I acquired as Barracks Chief would lead me to much greater adventures. My one regret is I stayed so busy during my six weeks of basic that I never made it into town. I never saw the Alamo.

THE LAST SUPPER

After finishing basic, I was assigned to Keesler Air Force Base in Biloxi, Mississippi. One of my buddies, Woody from Montana, was also assigned to Biloxi. We had a 10-day leave and since Woody wasn't going home to Montana before heading to Mississippi, I invited him to come home with me.

Arriving at Keesler, Gene and Woody, Gene on
Beach, Painting of "Christ at the Door"

Before going in service, I had purchased a 1937 Chevy Coupe. There was a huge oak tree in my stepfather's side yard. Woody and I put a chain hoist in that tree and removed the Chevy's original six-cylinder motor. We replaced it with a 1955 Corvette V8 engine and a Lasalle transmission. At the end of our 10-day furlough, we drove that hot rod 900 miles from Graham, North Carolina, to Biloxi, Mississippi. We were the optimism of youth: young, brave and foolish.

In my off-duty time, I preferred to paint. I was on duty at night as CQ and started working on a painting. I have always found it easier to sketch it with a pencil before painting allowing me to get the perspective of the whole scene easier. The Charge of Quarters job is usually a 30-day stint. The job was sitting behind a desk and locked door to sign in or out late coming airmen as well as to tour the barracks every few hours to make sure they were secure.

I had started a 3 foot by 6 foot painting of "The Last Supper", the hands always being the hardest for me to draw. The Charge of Quarters job afforded me the quiet time to work on the hands. Between an occasional interruption and making my rounds, the hands required about eight hours to complete. By the time my shift was over, I had them completed, all thirteen pair and the picture was ready for oil.

Over the next year or so, I would take the painting out and work on it. The more I worked on it, the more I regretted drawing it on hard back poster paper instead of canvas. As it turned out, it would become my lifetime achievement in the art field. Over the years, I have painted some decent pictures, but nothing to match "The Last Supper". Immediately after I finished the picture, I took a snapshot of me holding it and sent it to my Aunt Carlene in Virginia. She is a retired marine. I finished it up by taking it to the Base Wood Shop and building a frame for it. Then I sent it to the good christian woman who kept me so for many years, Mrs. Bessie Smith. She joyfully hung it over her kitchen table where it would remain until her death nearly twenty years later.

Holding painting of Last Supper, Commanding
the ranks and performing drills

Before her death, I extracted a promise from Bessie to have the pictured
returned to me upon her passing. She agreed, but somehow, during the
settling of her estate, the picture went missing. After I returned home, I
set out to track it down, but to no avail. Several years passed, I considered
it a closed matter, never would I see my painting again. One day, just
a few years back, I received a cardboard tube in my mailbox. It was

addressed to me and it came from Aunt Carlene. Unfortunately, we had not communicated very much over the years even though we were always very close when I was growing up.

To my astonishment, I unrolled a black and white picture of the "The Last Supper". It was the picture I had sent her twenty years earlier. She had it blown up to 3 foot by 6 foot. What makes it such a happenstance is that she never knew I had lost the picture. Although it is not the original, I have a copy that's the same size as the original. The Lord works in mysterious ways.

I organized a drill team while stationed at Keesler. Since I seemed to be the most experienced, it fell to me to be the instructor. Thanks, Lackland, all that experience did help. We seemed to spend all our waking moments including the weekends on the drill field. The guys were tireless, and we improved daily. We got so good at it they started inviting us to different social functions to perform. Things were really starting to roll when I got transferred to Florida along with several other members of the unit. That was the end of the team, but it was great fun while it lasted.

CARS, KEYS, AND WATERFALLS

I was being transferred to the 52nd Airborne of the Strategic Air Command at Homestead Air Force Base in Florida. The coupe had a bad habit of jumping out of fourth gear, so I didn't want to risk driving it through the swamps of Florida. My journey was taking me where the sides of the road were non-existent, but alligators and water were everywhere. I would be driving through Ochachobee swamp and some of the most desolate country imaginable. Gas stations were a hundred miles apart. A broken-down car was the last thing I needed.

So, I traded my favorite toy for a Chrysler that seemed trustworthy. If you can find one today, a 1937 Chevy is going for $127.000.00. I should have had my crystal ball. After I made it through the swamps, I ended up trading the gas guzzling old Chrysler for a 1957 Ford. It turned out to be a pretty good car and got me from point A to point B.

Gene Checking the Oil, Stationed at Homestead AFB

I was at Homestead Air Force Base for a year. Homestead was located about sixty-eight miles south of Miami, twenty miles north of the Florida Keys in the community of Homestead. That put me about 150 miles north of Castro and in my way of thinking, a little too close. At that time, he was doing a lot of saber rattling and he mostly just shot off his mouth a lot. For the most part, we co-existed with very little trouble. Our satellite was taking the Kodak moments, so we didn't have to worry. The stress would come soon enough.

I met a girl through one of my barracks roomates shortly after arriving at Homestead. Her name was Reba. We talked a lot, but there was no chemistry for anything other than friends. And we became very good friends. She would invite me to her home for Sunday dinner. I thought the world of Reba and fell in love with her parents, Albert and Vee Rogers. I started calling her Aunt Vee and after a while became a regular at their table. I thought so much of my adopted parents I would inform Aunt Vee that Reba shouldn't be seeing a certain guy, because of his reputation. It really ticked Reba off and I sometimes got the feeling that Reba wished she had never brought me home. But I didn't want anything bad to happen to her and I believe Al and Vee appreciated my concern for her.

I have never been one to waste time. That's evident by the fact that I am attempting to finish this book at my age. I guess I am one of those people Kennedy was referring to when he quoted George Bernard Shaw, "You see things; and you say, 'Why?' But I dream things that never were; and I say, 'Why not?'" Whatever the case, an idle mind is the devil's workshop. Whoever said that first sure knew what he was talking about.

One of my interests is oil painting. While I will never be a threat to Van Gogh, Monet or Michaelangelo, I do enjoy the creativeness of the craft even to this day.

Vee and Albert invited me often to the small Baptist church just a few miles down the road from their home. It was made up of a congregation of some great people. Like most Baptist churches, there was a baptismal pool behind the pulpit. The pool had a huge solid white wall behind it, an artist's dream, and being ever the artist, I suggested that the pastor allow me to paint a huge waterfall that would give the appearance of cascading down into the pool.

Every Sunday after church I would spend about four hours working on the project. The congregation was well pleased with the outcome and even installed some red, green and blue flood lights which accented the colors and gave off a reflection in the water. Poor Michaelangelo-I can't even imagine painting the Cistine Chapel in twelve years.

I can still hear Albert repeating one of his favorite sayings "There but for the grace of God, go I". Reba had introduced me to people that would remain lifelong friends. Years later, they even traveled to North Carolina to visit after Judy and I were married. They were the greatest folks in the world.

Vee sent me a newspaper clipping about a baby alligator she found under a bush in her front yard. But last I heard, she died in a house fire; she was also a heavy smoker and they think a cigarette was the cause of the fire. Albert retired from from the concrete company he worked for, moved to upstate Florida, and bought a pecan farm.

I was still stationed at Homestead during hurricane season in 1960. Hurricane Donna was predicted to make landfall on September 10 in the Florida Keys with the wall of the storm in full force as it arrived in Homestead. Immediately after the Hurricane alert was issued, the nuclear loaded B-52's and the KC-135 tankers took off like a flock of birds seeking refuge to avoid damage. Overnight, the runway went from a booming base to what seemed like a ghost town. We were informed that Homestead would take a direct hit, service personnel were ordered to remain in the hallway of the barracks until the storm had passed. We were told not to be misled when the sun came out, that would be the eye passing over us. The eye of a hurricane is the calmest part of a storm and would be over us for 15-30 minutes before the rain and 80-100 mile per hour wind would resume. "Deadly Donna" pummeled the cinder block barracks from mid afternoon to the following morning with winds so strong that palm trees lay horizontal with the ground.

Homestead received almost 11 inches of rain and $500,000 in damages during Hurricane Donna. While a lot of cars were completely flooded and ruined, I had the forethought to move my car across the street to an L-shaped building. I pulled that car as close as I could get, right into the 45-degree angle of the building. When the storm was over, there was a little water in the floorboard but no serious damage, leaving a lot of the guys wishing they had done the same.

Those cinder block barracks were first class. They were cinder block inside and out with two men sharing each room. Always full of energy, I decided I would paint a SAC emblem on a wall of our room. The SAC, Strategic Air Command, emblem was originally designed in 1951 by Officer Robert Barnes. It has a background of sky blue with two blue-gray shaded clouds. On the blue background is an arm in steel armor coming from the lower right. The hand, clenched fingers showing, is gripping a green olive branch and three red lightning bolts. The blue sky represents the Air Force operations. The arm and armor are a symbol of strength, power and loyalty. The olive branch, a symbol of peace with the lightning bolts symbolic of speed and power, all qualities of the mission of the SAC. The emblem is bordered in yellow with the words "Strategic Air Command" in a banner along the bottom.

Sharing my plan with my roommate, he was all for it, so I went to work on an eight foot by eight foot space. The room itself was only 12 foot by 12 foot, this was going to be a massive display. I sketched the emblem on paper and then expanded the dimensions to the size I wanted on the wall.

Almost the entire wall was covered with the mural upon completion. Looking at my beautiful piece of art, I couldn't help but have a queasy feeling that our Squadron Commander would see it and make me paint over all my hard work. The feeling was soon squashed as not only did he rave about it, but he liked it so well, he invited the Base Commander over to see it. Much to my joy and relief of not having to paint over it, he also said it was a great piece of work. I hope the guys who followed enjoyed it as much as I enjoyed painting it.

Paintings by me: Strategic Air Command Emblem
painted on wall and picture of Christ

SOUTHERN WOMEN

I met this redhead when I was stationed in Mississippi. She was as southern as they come. Here are just a few things about southern women

- They know their weather report: humidity, humidity, humidity
- They know where to vacation: the beach, the rivuh, the crick
- They know everybodys name: honey, darlin, shugah
- They know their movies: *Fried Green Tomatoes*, *Driving Miss Daisy*, *Steel Magnolias*, *Gone With The Wind*.
- They know their religions: baptist, catholic and football
- They know the cities with their quaint southern charm: Chawl'stn, S'vanah, Foat Wuth, N'awlins and Addlanna.
- They know their elegant gentlemen men in uniform, men in tux, Rhett Butler
- Southern girls know their prime real estate———the mall, the spa, the beauty salon
- Southern girls know the three deadly sins———having bad hair and nails, having bad manners and cooking bad food.
- Only a southern girl knows the difference between a hissie fit and a conniption and you don't" have "them you" pitch" them.
- A true southern girl knows exactly how many fish, collard greens, turnip greens, peas, beans etc. It takes to make "a mess",
- Only a southerner can point out the direction of "yonder" like in "it's over yonder" or how long "directly" is as in 'going to town be back drekly' (directly)
- Every southern girl knows that "gimme some sugar" is not a request for that white granular substance in the bowl.

- If you are a southerner and want to help out a neighbor in grief the best gesture is a plate of hot fried chicken and a big bowl of potato salad. And if he has real problems add a large banana puddin"
- A true southerner grows up knowing the difference between "right near" and "a right far piece" which can be one mile or 20 miles.
- And a true southerner knows you don't scream obscenities at litlle old ladies driving 30 miles per hour on the freeway. You just say "bless her heart" and go your own way.

Now if you happen to be one of those folks who are still having trouble with all this southern stuff, bless your hearts. I understand they are fixin" to have classes on southernness as a second language.

THE SAND AND THE SEA

My last two years in service were spent at Ramey Air Force Base in Puerto Rico, the servicemans paradise. When Ramey was operational, it had one of the nicest golf courses and officers's club in the world, the brass loved it there. Ramey was thirty-five square miles that included a hospital, swimming pool, shopping malls, theatres, and housing subdivisions. It was home to the 52nd bomb squad of General Curtis E. Lemay's Strategic Air Command. The base was on the end of the island in Aguadilla, the second dirtiest town in the world at that time. San Juan and San Turce were boom towns and ninety miles away at the other end of the island. The service boys at Roosevelt Roads had the luxury of that assignment. While in the service, I had sweated through the 100-degree weather of Texas and the long, hot oppressive days in Mississippi and Florida. But here in Ramey, the temperature stayed in the mid-70's most of the year with a constant breeze blowing in off the ocean, keeping it very pleasant.

Oldest Church in the New World, On Duty at Ramey AFB

The Church of San German Auxerre is the oldest church in the new world. It is located in San German (pronounced like Herman), the oldest town in Puerto Rico. The church was originally built as a convent in 1609 and became a church in 1688. Over the years, the church has been repaired and reconstructed after suffering earthquake damage but still retains its original beams. The church stands today as a museum of religious art, paintings and wooden carvings from the 16th century to current time. There are works from the Spanish, Mexicans as well as Puerto Rican people and is one of the most lavishly decorated churches on the island.

Ramey was a great duty. Ocean on both sides and coconut trees abound. We would climb the trees and cut the coconuts down, split them open with a machete and eat the meat from the center. Although partying on the beach was a rarity for me, I did enjoy taking the coconuts we had cut the meat from, filling them with rum and crushed ice and enjoying a very, refreshing drink. I was just never one for waste and had seemed to reach the point in life where partying was a waste of time, money, energy, and good health. As Robert Frost said "Two roads diverged in a wood, and I, I took the one less traveled by, and that has made all the difference."

Ramey had a radio station AFRS, Armed Forces Radio Services, and a complete elementary and high school system including a drama club with teachers from the states. Quite naturally I gravitated to both. With radio experience from my college days, I had no problem getting my own show. I also auditioned and won the lead role in a play being directed by Jim Brown, one of the drama teachers. He was from Illinois and he was under contract to the school system. I learned quite a bit from Jim about the theatre.

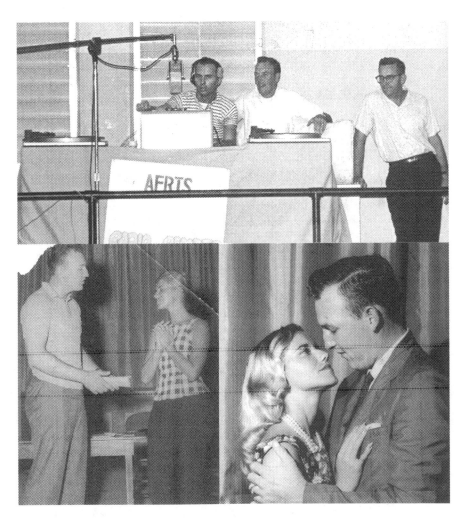

Armed Forces Radio, On Stage with the Drama Club

Gene at Sand and Sea, drawing off Duty, On
Duty at Dispatch, Enjoying a break

Jim was friends with Hal Hester, who served in the US Air Force. Hal
was a playwright and composer as well as a singer and nightclub owner.
He owned The Sand and The Sea in San Turce. If the name of the club
sounds familiar, it's because he went on to write the song by the same
name. The song was a smash hit recorded by Nat King Cole, selling more
than a million records. Hal also wrote and recorded an RCA album, *Hal
Hester Does His Thing*. Jim and I had been invited to the club and Hal was
a most gracious host, seating Jim and I at a front table and requesting one
of his singers sing *The Sand and The Sea* for us. Of course, Puerto Rico is
the rum capital of the world so we couldn't help but have a rum and coke
with dinner. And best of all, the tab for that excellent meal was picked up
by my new friend, Hal.

JOHN WAYNE'S IN PUERTO RICO

Between my nightly radio show and my endeavors with the drama club, I somehow found the time to purchase and care for a mare that was in foal. I rode her regularly until, on a stormy night, she foaled a palamino colt that I named Rayo, flash of lightning. He turned out to be a real looker.

There were several other guys in the squadron that had horses and we kept them all at The Bomb Depot. It was a great place for them, it had tons of grass that even grew on top of the bunkers. The Bomb Depot was five square miles of fenced, heavily guarded, dog patroled concrete bunkers that housed nuclear bombs. It was rumored that during WWII, the base had contained several underground missile silos for the "Truman Atomic Bomb". All through the Cold War era, Ramey was the staging ground for several covert military interdictions in Latin America. Since I had top-level security clearance access, it was not a problem to have the mare and Rayo in the depot. It also didn't hurt that I hit it off with our Squadron Commander a Major and former Marine.

Collection of 4 pics with Rayo and Mare at Ramey AFB

The Cuban Missile Crisis was a confrontation between the US and Soviet Union during the Cold War where the two came close to a nuclear conflict. During this time, the Soviet Union entered into an agreement with Cuban leader, Fidel Castro to put Soviet nuclear missiles in Cuba. Ramey was only a short distance across the ocean from Cuba and housed a base full of B-52's. During the Cuban Missile Crisis, Ramey went on the highest possible alert for a thirty-day period. During the alert, we worked twelve-hour shifts, rotating days and nights. The only thing we had time to do other than work was eat, sleep and get our uniforms washed.

The entire 35 miles of base was fenced in with a five-mile-long runway splitting it right down the center. The fences went all the way to the ocean on both sides. I would ride the mare all along the base lines and the fences.

During my rides, I noticed that along the fence line, there were far too many entrance areas, open holes and even places where the fences were completely down.

I knew that the problems along the fence line would be an open invitation for the nationalists to do some serious damage to our aircraft, so I took my concerns to the major, advised him of my findings and the security situation they imposed. I explained that with the twleve or so horses in the squadron, someone should ride the fence line and mark the location of the holes and the downed fences. The information could then be given to maintenance for immediate repair. There's an old service cliché; if you suggest it, you will probably end up doing it. He thought it an excellent idea, and that one man would be able to handle it and recommended I be the man to handle the job. I knew how important it was to secure our base, so I agreed to volunteer. Much to the envy of my fellow squadron horsemen, I was the one that got to play John Wayne for the next month. It was a worthwhile endeavor and I was doing what I loved. Every morning at 0700, the major assigned a truck to pick me up. I carried my saddle, M1 Carbine and .38 service revolver. They would drive me the twelve miles around the runway to the Bomb Depot. The kitchen always packed rations for my lunch. Along with my weapons and food, I carried maps and pens for marking the security breaches to repair. I was riding 8 to 10 miles a day and after a few days, I could tell it was taking a toll on my horse. Some of the other guys cowboyed up and volunteered their mounts. I had a remuda of horses and I knew my horse was grateful for the rest. Occasionally, if I was lucky, I would run across the coffee truck as I headed out to ride the fence. It made daily rounds to keep the guys awake and alert and riding the fences, I needed all the caffeine I could get. When I would come in from riding the fences, one guy or another would always ask "Well Duke, did you shoot any indians today?" I'd just grin and flip them the bird. I knew it was pure envy.

Sometimes, I would end my day and find myself on the opposite side of the base from the barracks. Normally, this would mean I'd have to ride an extra twelve miles around the runway to return the mount to the Bomb Depot. Luckily, the major believed in my project 100%, and had instructed the air traffic control tower to watch for me and give me the green light when it was clear. I would cross the the width of the runway instead of riding the extra miles around. At the end of the day, the other guys may have had aching feet but I had an aching butt and I was fortunate to have the major behind me, no pun intended. He was head of security for the base and carried a lot of clout especially at this particular juncture. I am probably the only person in the history of the base to ever cross Ramey Air Force Base's runway on horseback.

The more I rode the fences, the more I realized how important this project was. Some of the holes I found in the fence were big enough to drive a truck through. On many occasions, my day ended, sitting on horseback, watching the sun melt into the ocean, in the beautiful carribean. Those days, I almost forgot about the constant danger I might have been in from a sniper bullet.

The major was just as concerned about securing our base as I was. Every day I turned in my report, instructing maintenance of the issues and every day, the major had the crew out there repairing where I had marked. He was the man with the power to get the job done.

My family wrote often, keeping me apprised of the goings on of everyone and the happenings of our little Alamance County town. My sister Peggy was always very levelheaded about things growing up, always grounded and firm in her beliefs. I remember, she loved her little house. We referred to it as the peach house because the inside was decorated in shades of peach. Peggy was raising two kids in the small home and it was always full. I used to ask her why she didn't build a new one and her answer was always "I'm sending my boards to heaven for my home up there". I know she's now enjoying her house "up there" and I look forward to the day I get to sit down at her table for one more feast.

This particular letter started out as most of the others: "We miss you at Sunday dinner... hope you are safe". She concluded this letter with a poem. As I read it again, I find it is just as appropriate today, possibly even more so. Thanks Sis for being there for me:

Peggy, my Guardian Angel

When you get what you want in your struggle for self
And the world makes you king for a day
Just go to the mirror and look at yourself
And see what that man has to say

You may fool the whole world down the pathway of life
And get pats on your back as you pass
But your final reward will be heartaches and tears
If you've cheated the man in the glass

Six to eight months later, I requested a transfer to the Base Police. The major commanded both divisions and granted the request, where I worked the gates and drove patrol for several months. He then promoted me to dispatch, since he knew I was no stranger to the microphone as I was still broadcasting at AFRS.

The office that dispatch operated out of was inefficient so in my spare time, I drew up plans to remodel the office. The major agreed it would be a huge improvement when I presented the plans and once again, I volunteered to do the work. The major took me off patrol and regular duty so that I could go at it full throttle. I felt the dispatcher's desk should be at a higher level, so I raised the floor and built cabinets and storage spaces to house books and daily logs. The storage space included an inset for the dispatcher's typewriter and microphone. Directly across from the desk, in full view of the dispatcher, I designed a sliding plexiglass map with three layers that included blown up sections of Ramey, allowing the dispatcher to see the housing areas, the road, and the air field. The major was so pleased he gave me another stripe. Once the remodel was complete, I went back to the desk as dispatcher.

I made friends with a sergeant who was a boom operator on a KC-135 Refueling Tanker. I was scheduled to be off duty for the next 24 hours and he was scheduled to head out to Florida on a refueling mission. I was constantly telling him that his work seemed to be a lot more interesting than my desk job, so he asked if I wanted to come along. I jumped at this once in a lifetime chance. He cleared it with his captain, and we were off.

Boeing KC 135, Neighbor with K-9, Stateside with K-9, and Rayo

At the rear of a KC-135 is a huge glass bubble. The bubble is wide enough to house two couches and a boom. The boom has controls between the two couches. I took my place on one of the couches and listened through my headsets as my buddy chatted back and forth with the pilots. It was a clear, starry night and looking out through the bubble, we could easily see 5 miles to the B-52 that we would be refueling. We were over the coast of Florida when the Captain came over, "Will you tell that B-52 to get the hell up here. I've got a date tonight and I need to get back." My buddy looked at me, grinned and just shook his head.

When it was time, the boom was lowered unti it locked into position and with precision skill, the pilot of the B-52 eased the nose of that bomber right into the nose of the boom; it was like magic when it locked into place. I heard the B-52 pilot in my headset, "Ok, Mac, fill 'er up and clean the windshield. The oil should be fine." My buddy laughed, "Roger that, sir." The boom releases fuel at a rate of 1000 pounds per minute at 600 miles per hour. The pilot broke away from the boom and continued on his way as we made our way back to Ramey. It was the most exciting experience I had ever encountered.

I remained at the desk until I mustered out. When my contract with the military was over, the major offered me one more stripe if I would re-up, but I was longing for civilian life, so I headed home.

Before I was discharged, I sold the mare. I brought Rayo along with a K9 security dog back to the states with me. The K9 kennels were also located in the Bomb Depot and while visiting my horses, I was allowed to work with the dog often. I would visit him most days and we bonded. I had been sending Mom a little money along to have a pen built complete with overhead wire. The dog had been trained as an alert and attack dog and I wasn't exactly sure how the dog would adjust to civilian life. I didn't want mom to have any trouble with the neighbors if the dog got out of the pen even though I knew he went through de-programming and he was not dangerous. Had I thought otherwise, I would never have shipped him home.

I can't remember the dogs name. But it was the first of a long line of shepherds I've owned over my lifetime.

THE RAMP RAT

This is a 60 year old article I wrote one night on duty at Ramey. I thought of including the original handwritten manuscript, but didn't want to subject you to the torture of trying to read my writing.

How do you begin an article when you are forced to write in the dark? Without a light, it is most difficult, but a light is out of the question. It's been a long and difficult night as most midnight shifts are. But thoughts reach you during these hours are fleeting and will not return, so you must write them now. As was once so aptly put, "These are the times that try mens souls". This composition is strictly forbidden on duty, but it must be recorded in its original atmosphere. A truck comes by and I stop, possibly to lose an important thought. Picture, if you can, the conditions and imagine the night with a gray sky and twinkle of a scattered star. The dark and dreary runway is alive only with the reflection of lights on the wet ramp. An occasional bird with an eerie chirp or the early morning crow of a rooster from a distance, as destiny dictates to him, blends with the quietness. Our job is to guard aircraft and we are classified as Air Police 77150, or security branch, most commonly referred to as Ramp Rats.

This is our duty and around the clock, constant vigilance is a necessity. The statement best used to describe our purpose is "We guard SAC, so SAC can guard the world." To most people, this is just a melodious meaning and I suppose there are times when, even to us, it's just words, until we actually realize why we are here. There are no hours as long as ramp hours and no job quite as thankless. We are underpaid for the risks which, though questionable by some, do arise. So in such surroundings the question is raised, why? Why are we here? All over the world wherever our defenses are stationed we are present. In the rain and snow, in the sleet and hail, and in the hot, unbearable, heat of the dry days. Why? Why are we here? Is it actually answerable in a words or sentences? Is it strictly for the honorable discharge or our obligation of service to our country? To you my fellow ramp rat, I say this. When these questions are raised, stop and ask yourself. How far would those aircraft get if something happened without me here and how many people might tinker with those aircraft if there wasn't a security force?

So the ramp pounding continues and your feet ache and muscles get stiff and sore. There's no such thing as a holiday for security, for it never ceases. Why are my thoughts so versatile? Is there something in this soul that still cries out for sense of duty to guard our freedom? As the dawn seeps through a cloudy sky and it's almost relief time, the question again returns. What have I done or how much did I accomplish? And I realize in the outline of the pink sunrise and contrasting clouds is the nose of a steel blue bird, which in its rivoted frame silence says that "My country 'tis of thee" for which I was ever vigilant.

So let us always do today the things which our children will be proud of tomorrow, and let them never take for granted that which is given them, for it is so truly quoted "The price of freedom is eternal vigilance."

When the time comes that you feel like saying "to hell with it" without any outstanding extra "esprit de corps" or without being a sentimentalist, just tell yourself ramp rat, why you are here. And if your fellow man asks you your job, just tell him you stay on guard, so he can sleep in peace. And think also on this; your job is no less important than the guy who flies that plane, for his job is useless if that plane is rendered inoperable. Often the going is rough and the complaints are frequent. But always remember deep inside, that when they really need us; we know we'll be there. We will be there for the same reason our fathers and their fathers were there; that common something inside every individual that has participated in the greatness of the United States and will continue its participation as long as America exists. The price of freedom––eternal vigilance. God help us keep up our guard.

Signed – The Ramp Rat

B-52 Stratofortress at Ramey AFB

MILITARY FLAG FOLDING 101

You learn a lot in the military. One of those things the general public probably doesn't think about is how to properly fold the flag. It looks easy when you watch someone, but believe me, it isn't. It takes practice to get it to come out just right. You're never at a military funeral and see the officer stop midway, unfold the flag and start over. The reason that doesn't happen is that you practice so much, you can fold it in your sleep.

Every fold of the flag has special meaning. Here is Military Flag Folding 101.

The flag is meticoulsy folded 13 times. You may think it is for the original 13 colonies, but it's not.

The 1st fold is for the symbol of life

The 2nd fold is the belief in eternal life.

The 3rd fold is in honor and rememberance of the veteran departing our ranks, and who gave a portion of his or her life for the defense of our country to attain peace throughout the world.

The 4th fold represents the weaker nature, for as American citizens trusting in God, it is to him we turn in times of peace as well as war for divine guidance.

The 5th fold is a tribute to our country for as Stephen Decatur wrote "Our country, in dealing with other countries, may she always be right, but right or wrong she is still our country"

The 6th fold is where peoples hearts lie, with their heart they pledge allegiance to the flag.

The 7th fold is a tribute to its armed forces who serve to protect against all enemies foreign and domestic.

The 8th fold is for the one who entered into the valley of the shadow of death, that we might see the light of day.

The 9th fold is a tribute to womanhood and mothers who molded the character of the men and women who serve this great country.

The 10th fold is a tribute to fathers for he too has given sons and daughters in defense of their country.

The 11th fold represents the lower portion of the seal of King David and King Solomon and glorifies the God of Abraham, Isaac and Jacob.

The 12th fold represents the emblem of eternity and glorifies God the father, the Son and the Holy Ghost.

The 13th and final fold which leaves the flag completely enclosed with the field of stars uppermost reminding us of our nation's motto "In God We Trust"

These traditions and ways of doing things have deep meaning and I hope in the future you will remember this when you see a flag being folded.

Did you know that the 21 Gun Salute stands for the sum of the numbers in 1776, the year of our independence?

HOME REMEDIES OF LIFE

I had a limited amount of training in the medical field while in service; I was qualified to give CPR. Over the years, I've learned of a few things, home remedies if you will. You may find them handy in your life.

- Avoid cutting yourself when slicing vegetables by getting someone else to hold the vegetables while you chop.
- You can avoid arguments with females about leaving the toilet seat raised by simply using the sink.
- For high blood pressure sufferers–Simply cut yourself. After bleeding for a few minutes, it will reduce the pressure on your veins. You may want to use a timer.
- A mouse trap placed on your alarm clock will prevent you from going back to sleep after you hit the snooze button.
- If you have a bad cough, take a large dose of laxatives, You may still need to cough, but you will be afraid to.
- You only need two tools in life—WD 40 and duct tape. If it doesn't move and should, use the WD-40. It it shouldn't move and does, use the duct tape.
- If you can't fix it with a hammer, you have an electrical problem.

And if the above didn't make you smile, here's a parting thought: Some people are like slinkies, not really good for anything, but they bring a smile to your face when pushed down the stairs.

CHAPTER 3

MY LOVES COME TOGETHER

I was Back in Radio
Dream on Little Dreamer
The Most Powerful Loves Keep Coming Back
The Old Rebel and Pecos Pete Show
The Streak
The Hunters are Farmers
Bubblegum George
Bowling for Headstones
Breakfast with the Governor
Field of Dreams
Showboy
Princess and the Cart
God's Flashlight
I Fed the Cows, Did I Feed the Kids

I WAS BACK IN RADIO

I was late in life settling down. I understand today's young people taking longer to find their niche in this old world even though I must admit that I was a bit envious of others who always seemed to know exactly what they were to become. I had friends in high school who knew early on that they wanted to become a doctor, lawyer, accountant or teacher. That was not the case with me. I guess if I had been born in the 17th century I would have been an explorer. I was never satisfied and constantly searching wanting to try it all on for size just to see if it would fit. Now that I look back, I realize that I have learned one thing through life that is an absolute, nobody gets it all.

After I was discharged from the Air Force, I came back home to Graham, North Carolina to live with Mom and my stepfather, George Vestal. I loafed around for a couple months and tried to adjust to sleeping past 6:30 before deciding it was time to go to work. My mother was beginning to think the same thing.

While I was in service, Mom and George had built a new house a short distance from the 100-year-old homeplace they lived in when they got married. The homeplace was built by George's grandfather, Sherman Vestal. Sherman was named after General Sherman.

The Vestal Hotel

George's family had a great deal of history in Alamance County. The family also owned the Vestal Hotel, on the court square in Graham. The hotel opened in January 1903 but burned in July of the same year. It was rebuilt in 1904 with the same building that's standing today. The picture shows the original hotel with the balcony. Of course, it's been remodeled and changed hands numerous times. During one renovation, the bottom corner of the hotel was removed so cars could actually pull into the building to be fueled up. The second story of the building was held up merely by supporting beams and corner braces, and those original walls are still there. Tenants other than the hotel and the service station have included the United States Postal Service, Isley's Grocery, Riverside Café and Rich's Café. The Vestal Hotel is listed on the National Historic Register. You can see in the picture, the bus pulled by horses and mules. I can only imagine it was headed to the community of Ossipee for some kind of shindig.

George sold the old homeplace. Since, it was also listed on the National Registry, the purchaser had to remodel and couldn't demolish it. After purchasing it, the new owners put a lot into it. They've paved the drive and added a detached two car garage. Now it is a beautiful southern mansion with a wrap around porch and a screened in back portico. I remember coming home on leave and staying there and listening to the sound of the rain pitter pattering on the metal roof. There is no other more soothing sound in the world. I always slept like a baby in that house.

I began my professional broadcasting career at a local radio station WFNS. Later it became WBAG.

Blue Grass was extrememly popular then and there were two blue grass stars on the radio, Jim Hall on WFNS and Glenn Thompson on WBBB. They each had a band, a Cadillac and an enlcosed trailer to haul their musical instruments. They would travel around North Carolina performing their shows and then the next morning be back on the radio pulling their shifts. It was really a win, win for them. On the radio they covered a ten-county area so when they headed out to perform their concerts, they already had a fan base.

Glenn and Jim both did live studio music as part of their programs, so they had a pretty good thing going. I believe Glenn's theme song was "When You Sit and Think of Dixie" but my memory is fading and I can't remember Jim's theme song, even though I worked with him longer. The station's format was divided into hourly segments and the show playing on the station at any given time was dependent on the demographics listening just then. Bill Diffee might wake you up at 6:30 with some contemporary music. I would follow at 8:30 and play upbeat, soft rock until 11:00, then Jim would follow along after me at noon with bluegrass. Someone else would come along with easy listening for the rest of the evening. The whole concept was to satisfy the taste buds of the entire family. When digital radio came out, it extended the number of frequencies and stations multiplied expeditiously, programing became more infinitely specific.

Before there were any kind of prerecorded commercials, they were all live. A lot of times, the script of your presentation was in the hands of the copy girl or scriptwriter. You may be on the air with a program and get handed what's called an insert. It was a high traffic day with lots of commercials when I was given a commercial on the spur of the moment. I took the copy and commenced to reading it aloud while the music was playing. I noticed the copy girl was exceptionally quiet and I thought she was just listening to me proof it. She had made an error in the copy and I aggrevatedly exclaimed "Hell, I can't read this, it isn't right". She started repeatedly using the "Cut Throat" sign, the sign used to tell you to kill the mike. When I had taken the copy from her, I had forgotten to turn the mike off. I guess the music drowned out most of my verbiage, because I never heard anything from it.

We had a jock working at the station whose name was Tom, his air name, Tiger Tom. He was nuts, like most personalities in radio. It had been proven that the nuttier they were, the more they were listened to. He was good and later went on to a larger market in Charlotte at WBT or WSOC and was a huge hit with the truckers. He may have been an absolute nut, but he was a terrific jock. We became friends and after I got into television, I would drop by the radio station to sit in on his show. It would give him a break to use the John or stretch his legs. Sometiimes, I would read his newscasts for him. The studio was on the second floor of a building on Maple Avenue. It had a sound booth where the announcer would broadcast and a separate glass wall studio for interviews and live casts. In the studio, there was a table with a mike and kill switch. Tom could see me through the glass wall.

At that time, (You will note my use of that phrase numerous times in this book. So much has changed) we got our news from UPI, United Press International. It came off a teletype machine that typed continuously twenty four hours a day. Each story had a dateline and was typed in paragraph form with spaces between each story. The machine continuously fed the stories off in rolls. When you read it, you would start at the top and roll the paper through your fingers until you had read all the way to the bottom. Helping Tom out, I opened the mike and began reading the five minute newscast as I sat at the desk with my back to the door. In my peripheal vision I swear I saw the door open and close behind me but I continued reading the news uninterrupted. On hands and knees, Tiger Tom had very quietly crawled under the table and commenced to light a match to the bottom of my news copy. Talk about a hot news story! If you are a professional, you are a professional. In a split second, I killed the mike, stomped out the fire, flipped the mike back on and finished the broadcast. By then, Tom was back in the studio on the console. I could hear him laughing through the sound proof glass.

Opportunities for more air time or a nice increase in salary were always prime motives for movement in broadcasting so I went to work at WBBB, where Jim Isley, the man who orginally got me interested in this crazy livelihood, was working. A short time later, we had Bill Huff join the staff. WBBB was doing a lot of live church broadcasts. I was assigned to take Bill and the remote equipment to a church that Sunday. I showed Bill the procedure; plug in the console mike, hook up the two phone line wires to the small box where the two wing nuts were located, and open the volume meter. I said, "Bill it's 10:45. At exactly 11:00, you open the mike, and ride the volume meter so the meter does not peak in the red. I will be back to pick you up at twelve." To this day, Bill still talks about the extensive training Gene Hunter gave him. Welcome to broadcasting, Bill.

I had saved a fair amount over the four years I was in service and the first thing I did when I returned was buy a 1956 Ford pickup. There was a house for sale a few miles from my parents and while they didn't mind me living with them, I wanted my own place and privacy. Once I went to work in radio, I managed to put enough money away to visit the bank and work out a loan on the 1200 square feet house, four acres of land and a barn. I paid $17,000 dollars for this, my first home. My, how our sense of value has changed.

I began doing minor remodeling on the house, but it just seemed like the more I tore out, the worse it got. It was an old house with graphite shingle siding and hand sawed 2 x 4's, no two of them the same size. The floors were sagging and in such disrepair, I finally decided to tear it down to the foundation and start over. I braced the old floor with additional footings, poured new concrete and doubled the floor space to 2400 square feet.

I went to Sears Roebuck and opened a charge account to purchase a thousand dollars worth of tools. It was one of the hardest things to do in life, to get out of debt with Sears. I bought a Craftsman skillsaw and some sixty years later it's still getting the job done so, they do have great tools.

DREAM ON LITTLE DREAMER

When I entered television broadcasting, I envisioned myself as an anchorman on the news. I knew it would take a lot of experience and between college, Armed Forces, and commercial radio, I already had about six years in broadcasting at the time. I started my television career at WFMY-TV, a CBS affiliate in the position of booth announcer. The booth announcer handles voice-overs for the programming throughout the day. The position also included doing the weekend weather as "on the air talent". The weather wasn't nearly as sophisticated as it is now. The weather was gathered via phone from the Friendship Airport, known then as the Greensboro-High Point Airport. Thirty minutes before air time, we would call them and get the latest weather statistics. We had a triangular shaped board mounted on a spiral designed to rotate with your hands. Each side of the triangle had different statistics on it depending on your presentation. One side had weather patterns, another side had forecast, etc. Broadcasting had a unique training system. I call it the Nancy Pelosi technique; Do it first, then figure it out. I had no experience in weather reporting or its terminology but I had the weather line number at the airport, I'm a quick study and when you are in show business, you are expected to perform. So, l winged it until I knew it. My poor audience.

Gene as weather man, Singing at Pageant, Booth Announcer

I think my greatest screw up was when I forecast the next day to be sunny and warm. A friend of mine took his girlfriend on a picnic and it snowed. Oh well, that's show business! It took a long time for me to hear the end of that one.

One of the photographers brought his son to the station. He was a cute six-year old and I've I always loved the youngsters, so I asked if he wanted to sit on my lap in the booth and watch the monitor. Of course he did. All of the voice-overs were scripted in a huge book in front of me, the mike switch built into the console. Billy had been given strict orders by his father to be quiet and follow my instructions but kids are inquistive about everything. He was asking about this page and that control. He was watching me hold down the mike switch for some of the voice-over promos. He asked me about the page with the *Wizard of Oz* promo on it. Being funny, I asked him if he has seen the Wizard of O-Z? Billy had his hand on the mike switch at the same time the director yelled "Booth!" in my earphones. The voice-over promo went over the air waves as the *Wizard of O-Z*. I had a tough time explaining that one, but I never told his father what really happened.

I received an invitation to be the Master of Ceremonies for the Miss Graham Beauty Pageant. I was always ready for new experiences, so I accepted. Some beautiful young women were in the contest, so it wasn't exactly an unpleasant assignment. I rented a tuxedo from TN Boone Tailors on Main Street and proceeded to join in on the rehearsals. One requirement as Master of Ceremonies was to provide some form of talent during the intermission in order to give the girls time to spruce up in their evening gowns. I decided since the Jaycees had hired a small band, I would perform a solo. The day before the event, the band and I rehearsed a song that seemed to fit my range pretty well and had very few high notes, "Dream on little Dreamer". It was a Sinatra style song so when it was time, I announced that the band and I had prepared a little tune for them. In true Sinatra style, as the lights lowered, I walked on stage with a small stool and the mike and as I started to sing, I sat down. My sister Peggy was in the audience and I thought she would have a heart attack. She didn't even know I could sing, and to be honest, I wasn't too sure myself. There were no agents waiting at the door at the end of the night to sign a recording contract, but it wasn't half bad (or so my sister told me). Being young and in the entertainment business, I was game to try almost anything, God watches over fools and children. You have to leave your insecurities at the door in the entertainment world.

THE MOST POWERFUL LOVES
KEEP COMING BACK

Between my job and the construction of the house, I had dated a few times, none of which ever became anything serious. I hadn't seen or talked to Judy since enlisting in the Air Force six years earlier. I had heard some news about Judy's marriage and that she's back home living with her parents along with her three beautiful children; Marcy-4, Russ-2, and Julie-6 months old.

Judy and I started seeing each other three months after she moved back home. I have always loved children and fell in love with these three immediately. I had also always loved Judy and those kids only increased my love for her. There is a sign in my office that I have embraced all these years. It says "any man can be a father, but it takes someone special to be a daddy". With God's help, I have tried to live up to it.

When I got back from Ramey, I brought Rayo with me and boarded him at George's. Rayo was a Paso Fino and the breed is normally a small breed. Rayo was too small for me to ride so I hired a teenage boy to ride him and keep him exercised. The boy had taught Rayo to rare up, a habit of which I was never able to break him. I didn't want Judy getting hurt and she wasn't too keen on riding him with his nasty habit. I felt I was left with no alternative than to sell my Puerto Rican pony.

Since she loved horses almost as much as I did, I wanted her to have one. Earlier in the year, I had bought a gray, half Arabian horse, Gander at a riding stable in Greensboro. By inheritance, Gander was very intelligent. He had been broke in as a cow pony on a cattle ranch. Greensboro was about 25 miles from home, and I decided to ride him home. Gander and I were both glad when that ride was done. The exhuburence of youth.

My horse was boarded at Georges and when I told George my plan of a horse for Judy, he agreed to make the trip with us to the horse sale in

Siler City. Having George's experiences with the horses he had purchased in the past, we felt a bit more comfortable buying there. We found a racking horse, which we later named Racker, admittently, not a hard name to come up with. Racker was a spirited horse and Judy a fair rider, but she decided she could handle him. George chimed in and said, "That's a crazy horse you better leave him alone" and then in an instantaneous breath "aww... hell, go on and ride him, you can handle him". George would have made a great politician.

I had ridden Gander in numerous horse shows performing in barrel racing. He wasn't a large horse, but very muscular and because of his size, he could easily lay into the barrels. This increased his time giving him a split-second advantage over a larger animal. Gander had done it so many times, he could have run the barrels with his eyes closed. He knew the pattern better than I did and all I really had to do was hang on. Barrel racing was an event I enjoyed.

Judy had been wanting to ride Gander for a while. Walter Andrews was a good friend that had installed a regulation riding ring at his home so he could host events. Judy and I had taken the kids to Walter's and Judy decided that after the show was the perfect time to ride Gander. She just wanted to ride him about the perimeter of the fence at a leisurely lope. Our mistake was that we failed to let Gander in on what was going on. I helped Judy on the horse and she gathered the reins. As soon as she clucked at Gander, he bolted straight for the barrels, running his pattern. Judy had watched me race the barrels enough to know what was happening and that the only thing she could do was hold on tight. She managed to stay on for the entire pattern, but when Gander was finished, she quickly dismounted, handed me the reins and said "He's definitely your horse!" She refused to ever get on Gander again.

On September 10, 1966, I stood beside the woman I had been in love with my entire life. We were at her parent's home, surrounded by our families, as well as Marcy, Russ and Julie. It's hard to explain the way I felt when we exchanged our vows, promising to spend the rest of our lives together. I can only say I felt complete.

THE OLD REBEL AND PECOS PETE SHOW

Later in the year Judy bought me a beautiful Palamino, Dude, his hair still slick from his summer coat, for $300.00, a lot of money back then. I purchased a brand new saddle, bridle, blanket and breast plate from Sears for the astronomical fee of $97.33.

There was a program that WFMY aired in the sixties, *The Old Rebel and Pecos Pete Show.* George Perry played The Rebel and Jim Tucker was Pecos Pete. The program aired at 10:00am daily. It was a kid's show, along the lines of Howdy Doody (for all you elderly readers). George would don different costumes depending on the theme of the show and Jim was always the cowboy with his six gun and rope tricks. Jim was very proficient in the skill of roping. He could make a circle with the rope and jump through it. Then spin the rope around him and any kids on stage with him. The kids loved it. One day, George and I were talking. I told him about Gander and how fine-tuned he was. Gander would plant all fours when he felt the weight come off the saddle. He would stand quietly when you mounted but then turned on the switch. No meaness whatsoever, even a kid could hold him and mine often did.

George invited me to bring Gander to the station and put him on the show. There were huge doors leading into the studio from the parking area so the cameramen could roll the cameras out to the parking lot. The parking lot was surrounded by a huge privacy fence and Gander was an easy haul. George and I decided I would do the narration while Gander did his thing. I had to bring someone to ride him. My first thought was my friend, Wilbur Coggins. He had recently broken his ankle and was in a cast up to his knee but when he learned what I had planned for him to do, he "cowboyed up", cast and all and rode anyway. Once upon a time being on television was a big deal.

Dude

That winter, the City of Graham had invited Pecos Pete to be in the Christmas Parade, so I offered to let Jim ride Dude, and boy was Jim excited. The morning of the parade, Jim met me at the house I was building. I let Jim take my truck and trailer, Dude was already loaded and ready to go. I wanted to be sure he got there in plenty of time to saddle up and get ready. I had borrowed a paint horse from a neighbor along with a used saddle and bridle so I could ride in the parade with Jim. The horse I borrowed had not been ridden in a year and was really full of himself. Graham was five miles up the road so I told Jim I would ride the horse and meet him there. I thought the ride into town would settle him down before getting into the crowds. Wrong! I got about two miles up the rode and the horse was chomping at the bit. I said "Ok boy, let's see what you got". He had plenty. After a mile of wide open running along the shoulder I deemed it wise to get off the busy road. I started going behind my neighbors houses. Not wanting to tear up their yards, I decided to slow the horse down to a walk. I pulled back hard on the reins. Why is he going faster?? That used bridle had broken. The bridle was hanging around his neck, while I hung

94

on to the saddle horn of a runaway horse that showed no signs of stopping. Fortunately, I was off the road. Unfortunately, in that day, every yard had a clothes line. I flashed back to the days of stick horses and toy guns and a cut lip. I knew what was in store. After hanging on the side of the horse like a plains warrior and averting three potential decapatations; I straightened up in the saddle. It was just in time to realize this paint was headed for a huge thicket of pine trees. Knowing how Brer rabbit turned out and that I had to be seen on air with a presentable appearance, I made an decision. I said "Horse, here's where you and I part company". And as he continued to pay me no mind and intent on showing me what he had, I jumped off. After I jumped off, I rolled forever. I felt the relief of a Hollywood stunt man with no broken bones. The horse came to a dead stop. Apparently even he had more sense than to go into that thicket.

I caught him with no problem, made a makeshift lead rope out of the reins and walked him back to the barn. As I watched that night at home on the news, I agreed with Jim that it was a very nice parade; aching muscles and all. I never again put a used bridle on a strange horse. A life lesson well learned.

THE STREAK

I was on the weekend team with Mark Combs, a retired military officer and Woody Durham, who later became the voice of the UNC Tarheels. Mark did the news while Woody took care of sports and I handled the weather. The camera crew was always trying to crack Mark up while he was on the air. He was always all business and the perfect gentleman. He had a very stoic personality and when the camera was on he was automatically Mr. Professional. It was a Sunday night with a small crew of engineers and technicians on duty, all men. One cameraman made a bet with another that he could make Mark laugh on camera. The cameraman took off all his clothes and proceeded to parade back and forth behind the camera. Mark glanced up from his script (no Teleprompters back then) and caught a glimpse of the naked cameraman. He lost it. With a quick apology along the lines of "Sorry folks, you wouldn't believe what just happened if I told you". He immediately regained his ususal composure and serious demeanor and continued on with the broadcast. Of course the cameraman won his bet, but probably regretted it the next day when the Program Director heard about it.

WFMY News Promo Pamphlet

I didn't get home until midnight most nights after driving thirty minutes to get home from work. I would wake in the mornings, eat quickly, and head out the door to work on the house four or five hours before heading to the television station. I did this everyday for a year and a half until the house was complete. It was worth every second as it turned out beautiful.

Eighty percent of the labor that went into the house was mine. Neal Smith, the Vice President of Mebane Savings and Loan gave me a construction loan, basically made on a handshake of six thousand dollars so I could finish the house. I had just driven the last nail in the four-bedroom three bath house on a 4-acre plot with a barn when a lady drove in the driveway and asked me if it was for sale. I told her I didn't build it for sale, "But what do you have in mind."

She lived in a ranch style brick home on 70 acres of land in Snow Camp. She was a nurse and her husband had severe heart problems so she wanted to move closer to the local hospital.

It piqued my interest, so Judy and I visited the farm. It had a nice brick home with a carport, a large old barn and a couple of outbuildings. After looking it over, Judy and I, a couple of excited kids decided to trade homes with the owner. Judy's mother thought we were crazy but we were young. We both loved and wanted horses and the thought of living in the country appealed to us both.

Reprinted with permission from WFMY-TV

THE HUNTERS ARE FARMERS

We moved to the farm with a little bit of furniture and a lot of dreams. Snow Camp has a great heritage dating back to the Colonial War when General Cornwallis named the area after camping there during a snowful around the time of the Battle of Guilford County Court House. It has a large population of Quakers and is home to an outdoor drama known as "The Sword of Peace ". The area is beautiful with lots of rolling hills, creeks, meadows and mountains. The topography is gorgeous and not unlike the landscaping in Gary Coopers movie, "Friendly Persuasion ".

We were greener than a new gourd when it came to farm living. But we loved the country and the farm and were both eager students. We decided to plant our first garden and called on the wisdom of my mother and stepfather to help. Under their tutelage and expertise', we excitedly planted our first garden. To us it was the garden of Eden. I think we planted everything known to man and possibly some things that weren't. Not yet having acquired a tractor, mainly due to lack of funds, one of our neighbors graciously cut up a chunk of land behind the house and then ran a disc harrow over it to make it ready for planting. He took a couple of tines off his cultivator and laid off the rows for us. For payment, Judy baked him an apple pie as he would have been insulted had we offered to pay him cash.

Everyone joined in and it really became a team effort. Even the kids were having a crack at mother nature, while George and Mom were conducting the classes. We learned how far apart to drop the seeds, how deep to cover them and which seeds to mound up and tap down. It was truly a work of art to a novice and it turned out beautiful.

Now all we thought we had to do was wait on God to work his miracles. Mom and George had forgotten to tell us that weeds grow as fast as plants and while we had hoes and three kids it was a huge garden. Even though funds were limited, our credit was good. We decided we were going to have to purchase a tiller. It was a Gilson which I kept for the better part of forty years. When I sold it, it was still running. I maintained it well and it fed the family for a lot of years.

Life on the farm is a learning experience and after a few weeks the corn, cucumbers and squash started popping up. The radishes popped their little shoots up. I had never used or seen anybody use a tiller before, but I thought "How hard can this be?" It seemed obviously simple too me. There were two sets of tines on each side of a chain driven axle which had a space of about six to eight inches in the center. Of course, that space was to give you enough room to till over the top of the plants, right? Wrong! Remember, I was a cowboy, not a plowboy as I rediscovered after having dug up about a half row of radish plants. Judy, being the smart one in the family quickly informed me she thought I should go in between the rows, not over them. That definitely worked better with no loss of plant life. That was the solution for me and the tiller for a lot of years; just listen to Judy. I've always been a quick study, but they should have put instructions on the cussed thing. Cowboys don't know anything about farming. Back then there was no book called Cultivators for Dummies. But I could have been the author after that experience.

From then on, everytime I would break out the tiller, much to her delight, Judy would say "Now Gene, remember, in between the rows" to which I would grimace and reply lovingly "Ok Sugar Babe, just remember these handlebars will fit even those small hands". She never replied but quickly disappeared into the house not to return until I put the tiller away.

BUBBLEGUM GEORGE

We began looking for a church home. Bethel Presbyterian Church was close to the farm, so we decided to visit. This being our first visit and not knowing anyone in the community we got all gussied up, that's southern talk for really dressing up. We headed out the door early so we could get a seat and pulled into the full parking lot a few minutes before the service was to start. We could hear the congregation singing a hymn. Not wanting to be obvious, we slid into the last pew and quickly joined in the hymn. As soon as the song ended, the pastor gave the closing prayer and dismissed the congregation. We had forgotten about Daylight Savings Time and hadn't changed our clocks accordingly. We had missed the entire service. The members of the church were very cordial and understanding of what had happened, but Judy and I were so embarrased we never went back. I guess it must have been God's plan for us not to join that particular church.

Once we got squared away on the farm, we would take the kids every Sunday to see George and Bessie. George always had bubble gum for the kids and in the following years, he was lovingly referred to as Bubble Gum George, so as not to confuse him with my stepfather, George. Their house sat down in a valley at the bottom of a meadow. Bessie could put Betty Crocker to shame with her cooking and was up every Sunday morning with the sun to begin cooking. Bessie prepared a huge meal and as the kitchen heated up from the stove, she who would open her kitchen window and her voice would drift out across the meadow for all the neighbors to hear. She made a joyful noise. Even passing cars were subject to hear her singing "Shall We Gather at the River". Then it was off to Riverside Baptist Church to hear the Riverside Quartet and the Oakley Family Trio. Bessie was a saintly woman and constantly raving about the beautiful music at the church. She convinced us to go with her one Sunday and after the service, we knew we had found our church home.

George liked to stay home after a hard week in the mill and watch wrestling and I had long since given up trying to convince him that it was fake. George had made a trip to South Carolina a few years back and had all his teeth pulled and replaced with dentures. It took him awhile to adjust to them. Older people seem to have that problem, I guess it's the permanent change that scares them. My family will laugh at this and say I'm the same way with my hearing aids. When George was at home, he would sit in his favorite lounge chair and when something would crack him up like Don Knotts on The Andy Griffith show, George would lean back in his chair and cackle, always making sure he covered his mouth as he only wore his teeth when he went out. It's strange, the things you remember about a person.

Bessie was never able to get George to go with her, but she prayed for him constantly. I am sure before he passed, he found the Lord. George lived long enough to see me on television, but he died from an aneurism while eating a pack of peanuts and drinking a Pepsi. Judy broke the news to me at midnight after I got home from anchoring the 11:00 news. I felt as though I had lost two fathers in my lifetime.

A few months after joining the Riverside Baptist Church, I met another man who has impacted my actions throughout my life. His name is Jesus Christ. When I opened my heart and let him in at the alter, my entire family joined. My decisions in life would forever be made in a different context and I knew from that day forward he would always be my rock. While I have let him down many times over the years, he has yet to fail me. I saw a bumper sticker "Christians aren't perfect, just forgiven". That pretty much sums it up. It's a tough world we live in, so if you are planning on getting through it, you are going to need all the help you can get. As the Duke so aptly put it "Life is tough, but its even tougher if you're stupid".

The kids loved the church and some Sundays, the three of them would sing to the whole congregation. I just made a joyful noise, but they carried a tune pretty well. Our pastor, Curtis Oakley, was the most caring, mild mannered God-fearing man I ever knew. His wife, Elizabeth, and children Jeff and Linda made up the Oakley Family Trio and produced an album. We were pleased to be members and Curtis was always there for his flock when any kind of tragedy struck. Judy and I spent many a night in prayer over our lives and the lives of the children. I do not for a minute doubt the results of those prayers.

BOWLING FOR HEADSTONES

We lived at the farm only a short time, when I was given the opportunity to be News Director and Anchorman at WITN-TV in Washington, North Carolina. It was a wonderful opportunity that we felt like we had to take so we found a family that wanted to rent the farm so we moved the family to the coast. We carried the kids, four horses, a dog and a military Jeep. We had rented an old house with some acreage and needed the Jeep for work purposes around the farm. It was late spring when we made the move, so we immediately planted a garden in the sandy soil of the eastern part of the state. It only took a few days for all the seeds to germinate. It was just amazing to me how quickly it seemed to happen in that sandy soil.

Monday July 24, 1967
Afternoon-Evening

⑧ [COLOR] NEWS, WEATHER, SPORTS
⑪ RIFLEMAN—Western
⑫ GUESTWARD HO!—Comedy
5:45 ⑤ SPORTS—Ray Reeve

Evening

6:00 ② ③ ⑨ ⑨ ⑪ ⑫ [COLOR]
NEWS, WEATHER, SPORTS, EDITORIAL
② ④ NEWS—Lentz, Faulkner
③ ⑤ ⑥ ⑦ ⑫ NEWS, SPORTS, WEATHER
⑧ MOVIE—Adventure
"Tarzan Finds a Son." (1939) Tarzan saves a baby in a wrecked plane and takes the infant home with him. Johnny Weissmuller, Maureen O'Sullivan, Johnny Sheffield, Ian Hunter. (One hour, 25 min.)
⑱ TROUBLE WITH FATHER
"The First Fight." Joyce and Jimmy have the first quarrel of their married life. Stu and June attempt to intervene, but they wind up having their own quarrel. Stu Erwin, June Collyer, Merry Anders, Sheila James.

6:15 ② ④ MERLIN THE MAGICIAN
③ MOVIE—Western
"Adventures of Gallant Bess." (1948) A cowboy captures and trains a wild mare. Cameron Mitchell, Audrey Long, Fuzzy Knight, James Millican. (One hour, 15 min.)

6:20 ⑤ [COLOR] NEWS—Peter Jennings
6:30 ② ③ ⑨ ⑪ [COLOR] NEWS
—Harry Reasoner
② ④ PATHFINDERS
Benjamin DeMott travels to Philadelphia to explore the career of baseball's Connie Mack, who devoted his lifetime to the sport.
⑥ ⑦ ⑨ ⑫ [COLOR] NEWS—
Chet Huntley, David Brinkley
⑫ ⑱ [COLOR] NEWS—Jennings
6:50 ⑤ VIEWPOINT—Jesse Helms

NEWSCOPE with Gene Hunter

See, as well as hear, the latest news developments in Eastern Carolina as Gene Hunter anchors "Newscope".

Monday - Saturday 6:00 P. M.

witn tv 7

Promo in the Cartwright Edition
*Reprinted with permission from WITN-TV

After living there six months we were disappointed to find we had rented our farm to the wrong people. They weren't paying the rent on time and at this point, we risked losing the entire farm to foreclosure. We made the decision to return home. Sadly, I turned in my two weeks notice and explained the situation to the owner of the station, Bill Robertson. He hated to see me leave, but he sympathized with our situation and even offered to loan me the company trailer to move our belongings. Judy had always hated living in Washington. So, after working one week of my notice, I loaded up Judy and the kids, along with all our belongings and made the trip back to Snow Camp. We owned at 1969 Ford Country Squire Station Wagon with a hitch on the rear. I loaded the Jeep, the last thing we had to move, and carried it back to the farm. I still had a week left to work on my two weeks notice, so, after unloading our belongings and getting everything squared away, I said goodbye to my wife and kids, and headed back to the coast, pulling the empty trailer behind me.

The thoroughfare to the beach was Highway 70 through Durham. It was a four-lane road with a median in the middle. It was ten at night as I passed the Wake Forest exit and rounded a curve. On my right was a huge cemetery. It was so big, it had a sizeable maintenance building sitting just off the highway down a sharp embankment.

I was in the left lane with the window down, singing along to country music on the radio. I was relieved to have everything back in its proper order and was enjoying the drive on a road with no traffic coming or going. I caught a glimpse, a flash of something passing me on the right and all I could think was "What fool is driving around this late with no lights on?"

It was at that instant that I realized what I saw. My trailer was riding in the right lane…. beside me. It was loose from the station wagon and headed down the embankment into the graveyard. If it weren't for it hitting the maintenance building, I would still be paying for headstones today. There was nothing to do except leave and deal with it the next day.

I headed to Washington, contacted someone in Raleigh the next day to weld me a new hitch then drove back and picked up the trailer. The station never gave me any grief about the accident and the episode of the runaway trailer concluded. Guess the good Lord didn't want any of those souls at rest to be disturbed.

BREAKFAST WITH THE GOVERNOR

WRAL-TV covers most of Eastern North Carolina. Jesse Helms was Vice President of WRAL-TV at the time and was doing his commentary "Viewpoint" as a sidebar piece. He was a household name in the eastern part of the state with his immensely popular program. He was famous for calling a spade a spade.

I contacted Jesse and set up an interview. They needed a reporter to cover the state capitol and he sent me to his news director and anchorman, Sam Beard. Sam had a voice that sounded like he was in the Holland Tunnel. He was a heavy smoker. I must have made a pretty good impression on him because Jesse called me the next day and offered me the job to which I immediately said yes. I mean covering the state capitol for television. I would have done it for free just for the experience.

I worked for Jesse, but my immediate day to day assignments came from Sam. I had jumped headfirst into the maddening world of politics and, boy was it a ride. Jesse had a huge following and he definitely had his viewpoint. He was elected to Congress numerous times because of his immense popularity. You either liked him or disliked him. Even after he became one of the most powerfull Senators in Washington, those who disliked him still tendered a great deal of respect for his opinions. The thing about Jesse was that you always knew where he stood on any given subject. It made him different from the capitol, full of hot air balloons, we have today. As a good friend used to say when referring to most politicians "You can't tell where he stands until he sits down".

Gene at Desk, Autographed Photo from Governor
Moore, In the Legislative building.
Reprinted with permission from WRAL-TV

When covering the State Capital for WRAL, there was minimal
security at the Governors Mansion, or Gingerbread House as it was
affectionately named by the news reporters. There were no fences or
security guards around the facility. North Carolina citizens could roam
the grounds freely with minor restrictions. Many times, on the beat I have
walked into the Governors office at the capital and exchange pleasantries
with the secretary. She would send me in to meet with the Governor. As
you can imagine, that kind of relationship with the press no longer exists.

One time, an invitation went out to all the capital correspondents. It was a breakfast with Governor Dan Moore at the Governors Mansion. That morning the crowd of newspaper, television and radio reporters filed through the front door of the mansion. Most of us knew each other, at least the local ones, so there was plenty of conversation. When we reached a large entrance hall, one of the houses emloyees directed us to the state dining room. We entered and gazed upon a fifty-foot-long dining table. It went from one end of the room to the other. As would be expected of a formal function, our place cards were on the table with the governor sitting at the head. He was a pleasant man, a country lawyer from the mountainous area of the state and a southern democrat. I was at the end of the table with the Governor, so most of the conversation seemed to be between me, the governor, the reporter seated next to me and the two reporters across the table. Of course, everyone was talking, so the room was noisy. The Governors wife was on a fact-finding mission in South America, so she was unable to attend.

There was a prominent legislator during that time who was a well know womanizer. This legislator was the head of the committee the first lady served on. In the course of the conversation, the purpose of the trip naturally came up. When the governor mentioned that she was traveling with this committee chairman, I opened my mouth and inserted my foot "I bet she's having a good time" there was an instant silence in the first eight or ten seats. The governor ignored the remark and so did my colleagues. Someone quickly asked a question about the budget to get over the awkward moment. When the meal was over, the governor graciously signed personalized pictures of himself for all the reporters. I made a point to be last. He had a devilish look in his eye, and I wasn't sure what was coming next. As he handed me the picture with my name on it, I was half expecting to see the words "Drop dead Gene Hunter". I graciously accepted the picture, offered the goverenor my profound apology and told him I did not mean for my remark to come out the way it sounded.

He put his arm around my shoulder, walked me to the front porch as the other reporters were filing out and said, as though I was a relative, "Son if I got upset over everything I heard in politics, I wouldn't be in politics. I've got thick skin". We had a laugh and a hearty handshake and I said as I walked away, I would see him at the capital on my next round.

FIELD OF DREAMS

Back on the farm, life returned to normal. After a year, we had saved enough money to buy a used tractor. We found an old John Deere 40. It was a hit and miss, called so because it sounded like it was constantly skipping when operating normal. The front wheels were sandwiched side by side instead of spread out. The tractor had a high metal seat and after a few hours you were ready to climb down. It wasn't running just right, but my brother-in-law, professed to be a mechanic. We were at the barn, which was a good distance from the house, and needed a tool out of his car. I volunteered to retrieve it. It took about five minutes to get back to the house, find the tool and make my way back to the barn. The road to the barn splits the pastures, cows on one side, horses on the other, crosses a creek and up a hill before it reaches the barn. I had just crossed the creek when I heard my brother-in-law yelling. The barn had no running water and the tractor was going up in smoke. I went flying up the hill, helping him throw dirt on the tractor which was fully aflame by now. Turns out he was testing the spark plug wire to see if he was getting any fire to the plug and got too close to a leaky carburetor. It was a total loss and with no insurance I was once again without a tractor. I sold the charred John Deere the next day to a local farmer for fifty dollars, who probably tore it down and restored it.

I had to make do for quite a few months until I found a good deal on the same model tractor Kevin Costner drove in the movie "Field of Dreams". After buying it, along with a bush hog, a plow and a cultivator, I was in farmers heaven. I was ready to thank my brother-in-law for making charcoal out of the first one. All was forgiven. This tractor was a cadillac and my nightly plowing now became a pleasure. I usually planted three or four acres of corn every year to feed the cows and horses. I kept my field of dreams tractor until we sold the farm and it never once failed to start. It is true, "nothing runs like a deere".

SHOWBOY

One of the many horses I owned over my lifetime was an American Saddlebred, Showboy. He was a beautiful sorrel with a white face and four white stocking feet. I bought him from a man in Siler City. As soon as I crawled up on him, I knew I had to have him. Whoever was supposed to have gelded him didn't complete the job, so he was still half stallion. Well, I was man enough, or foolish enough to think he had met his match. There had been very few horses I couldn't ride. As the old cowboys used to say "There's never a horse that couldn't be rode and never a rider that couldn't be throwed".

Showboy wasn't the kind of horse to take to just anyone. He didn't like strangers coming into his pasture, which I found out when I got him home. For whatever reason, he had bonded with me after I had ridden him. I could walk up to him, bridle him, crawl on him bareback and ride anytime. He had also bonded with Judy's horse, Tina which was to be expected. But anybody or anything else was fair game. He wouldn't even let a dog come in the pasture with him, He wasn't exactly mean, but he definitely had an attitude.

Judy and the kids were afraid of him and wouldn't have anything to do with him. Tina was a family horse and all the kids loved her. They were constantly petting her and feeding her apples. And evidently, Tina loved the kids just as much. We had the electric fence, which was about three to four feet off the ground. Julie knew not to touch it but was small enough to walk under it with no problem. Judy was in the house. The kids, as usual, were playing in the back yard and even though Julie had been warned not to go into the pasture with Showboy, she decided she wanted to feed Tina an apple. She proceeded to walk under the fence and head to Tina, where she fed her the apple and rubbed her legs. Showboy was about thirty feet away and saw what was going on. He started toward Julie and Tina with his ears layed back. Tina sensed what was about to happen and moved her haunches (rear end to you pilgrams) toward Showboys face. Julie was still standing between Tina's front legs when Tina layed her ears back giving out a screech. Judy, having heard this sound before when Tina didn't want Showboy near her, came dashing out of the house and ordered Julie out of the pasture just as Showboy backed off. I sold Showboy the next day.

Showboy

PRINCESS AND THE CART

The kids, Friends son on Princess

Judy and I both had horses and wanted to enjoy our acreage at the farm. Now, we just had to come up with a plan to ride with three kids. Marcy must have been around six by then. We found a two-wheel pony cart in Graham that a man had built. Judy and I talked it over and decided to buy the cart that very night. We tied the cart to the top of our Falcon Station Wagon and headed to the farm, three excited kids squealing for joy in the backseat. We didn't have a harness or a pony, just a cart. It was pitch black by the time we unloaded the cart but there is no containing the enthusiasm of a child and there was no going to bed until they rode in that cart. You don't have to be a rocket scientist to figure out who played horse that night. Using the lights from the floodlights that faced the driveway, here I was, pulling three screaming kids up and down the road.

We quickly found a set of harnesses and a sweet, gentle snow-white pony. The pony, Princess, served as both a cart pony and a mentor for each of the kids as they learned to ride. Our problem was solved. Marcy quickly learned to drive the cart and our whole motley crew were able to go riding often. I would take the point, Judy the drag, and sandwich the kids in their cart in-between. There were thousands of mountainous acres surrounding the farm and wherever the cart could go, we rode.

One bright sunny Saturday, we all saddled up to take a ride to the top of Cane Creek Mountain. I was on point, the kids in the middle and Judy at drag on Tina. Tina was a great horse with only one flaw, if she had not been ridden in a while, she was reluctant to leave the house. Judy was a gentle, sweet, soul and very few times in our forty-year marriage, did I ever see her upset. But this was one of them. It had rained the night before and there was a mudhole at the end of our driveway. I had led off with the kids right behind me. I looked back to check on things and Tina was going around and around the mudhole instead of standing for Judy to mount. I chuckled and when I looked back a second time, Judy was on top of a horizontal Tina down in the mudhole flailing the daylights out of her with a riding crop. Tina got up, stood still, and Judy mounted and proceeded to follow the procession. That was the first and only time in my life; I ever saw Judy hit an animal. Tina never again offered any resistance when leaving the house. You think horses don't have memories. Think again.

Our little caravan worked out well for several years until Marcy grew older and she wanted her own horse. We found a great little Paint mare, Sugar from the Elon Orphanage in Elon. Many kids at the orphanage had learned to ride on Sugar, and she seemed very gentle when we took all of the kids to visit, so we knew she would be a safe horse for Marcy. It was close to Christmas so Judy and I decided Sugar would be a surprise present. I hid her in the barn on Christmas Eve. The ground was covered with snow so we were pretty sure Marcy wouldn't go snooping around the barn and discover her. Early Christmas morning, after our annual Christmas morning breakfast, the kids were all playing with their gifts when I announced I was going to the barn to feed the cows. No one turned a head or even acted like they had heard me. Even Julie, our little animal lover, didn't seem to want to go. I had made a study table with built in pencil holders for Marcy's room and she was sitting at it when I walked out. I bundled up and headed out to the barn where I put the bridle on Sugar and rode her back to the house. Judy had brought Marcy out on the front porch when I rode up. She recognized her right away. I slid off the horse, handed Marcy the reins, and said "Merry Christmas, Sweetie". I didn't think we would ever get that child off that horse that morning, even in the cold snowy weather. I could relate because it reminded me so much of my first ride in the pasture at George's.

Marcy had Sugar, Russ rode Princess and Judy and I would take turns riding double with Julie. We no longer needed the cart and sold it and the harness.

GOD'S FLASHLIGHT

Late one evening we a had a severe thunderstorm, one of those summer storms that seemed to frequent Snow Camp. Judy no longer had Tina, instead she owned a horse named Nugget. Nugget was a beautiful Palamino who was scared to death of storms. The horse was so scared, I would have to stall her up if there was a lot of lightning. This storm had come up quick and as the evening wore on, it got worse. I donned my rain gear and headed out into a cold, rainy, stormy night to stall Nugget. Our horses were always good about coming when called, but after walking the entire fifteen-acre pasture and not being able to find them, I found a spot where the fence was down. Uh oh! I knew we were in trouble and hurried back to the house to inform a frantic family what I had found. All five horses were gone. Not wanting to leave the kids alone at night in a storm, we all piled into the cab of the pickup and started riding the dirt roads surrounding the farm. It was roughly ten square miles. It was looking for the proverbial needle in a haystack. If only GPS's were invented, and the horses had trackers. We rode around for what seemed like hours. Up one road and down the next. The Cane Creek Mountain range ran through the backside of our property with lots of trails. The main road, Greensboro-Chapel Hill Road, had a dirt road off it, Holman Mill Road that paralled the backside of our farm. We drove past the two-story farmhouse with its grown-up fields. The rain was still coming down in torrids and lightning was flashing all around us. With the children providing us three more anxious set of eyes, we were futilely looking into the darkness hoping for a glimpse of our lost companions.

We had decided to give up for the night and had just turned around in the old farmhouse driveway to head home. We drove back over that same stretch of road when a huge flash of lightning lit up the entire sky. It seemed to last forever and was like God was providing us a huge flashlight for the occasion. (irony: as I write this my power is out, I'm sitting on my front porch and its pouring down rain—-quite a mood enhancing backdrop) When the sky lit up, one of the kids screamed "Daddy, the horses" I slammed on brakes and looked out in the lighted field to see the most georgeous five horses I had ever seen.

I always kept a couple of ropes in my truck, so Judy caught Nugget and one of the other horses. I think they were as glad to see us as we were them. We couldn't leave them for fear we wouldn't be able to locate them again. So, Julie and Judy held the two horses in the storm while I took Marcy and Russ and drove back to the barn to retrieve the halters. I wasn't excited about the idea of leaving them out in the driving rain, but Judy assured me she and Julie would be fine. "Just hurry back" She urged, and boy, did I? It must have been around ten thirty and there was no traffic on the country road, so I drove as fast as I safely could. The kids and I hurriedly grabbed up the lead ropes and each horses halter. I was only gone twenty minutes, but it seemed an eternity to me and poor Judy and Julie. Remember now, that God was still providing the light show. Judy was probably wishing that God's batteries would go dead since she was covered with the light I left her. We got back to the girls and haltered all the horses. I put a cold, rain-soaked Judy and Julie in the warm cab of the truck and tied all the horses to the tailgate. It was a slow five mile per hour drive back to the barn. We put them all up in their dry stalls, which I'm sure was appreciated as much as our own warm, dry beds were to us. It was probably midnight by the time we turned in. As true cowboys would, we were so tired, we slept dirty that night, far too exhausted to shower.

I FED THE COWS, DID I FEED THE KIDS

We were always thinking of ways to make the farm pay for itself. The most obvious thing would be cattle. We started out buying "sucklings", baby calves that are still nursing which normally sell for $20.00 each, well within our budget. We invested in six, quart size, plastic bottles and six calf nipples. Our first sucklings were six Holsteins. Because of Holstein's markings, they are very hard to tell apart. We brought the calves home and put them in their stall, warmed their milk and Judy and I proceeded to feed them.

I had to work the next morning, so Judy and the kids oversaw the morning meal for the calves. Can you picture this? Three small kids, a german shepherd, and six small, hungry calves; it was a recipe for disaster and one morning meal I'm glad I missed.

I heard Judy's version when I got home, and it went something like this: "Julie was crying and didn't want to be out of my sight or away from my side. The dog wouldn't stop barking at the calves and the calves wouldn't stop bellowing for food. And all these calves look identical, so I kept getting confused as to which ones had been fed and which had not." I probably would have been rolling in the floor laughing my head off, if Judy had not been so frustrated and upset. She told me she had either fed six calves once or three calves twice, she just wasn't sure. I guess she got it right as they all made it to adulthood, even the kids.

After the Holstein fiasco, we switched to Hereford cattle. We bought a steer to raise and slaughter for food. Julie was our little animal lover and proceeded to make that steer her personal pet, even naming it Bully. Don't ever let a kid give a name to an animal you plan to eat. Julie loved that animal so much, she would go out in the pasture with that cow and while Bully was sunfishing (laying on his side with his belly toward the sun for warmth), Julie would lay on his belly and take a nap. The time came to slaughter Bully so we would have food to carry us through winter. Judy and I knew we were going to have a problem. We agonized over how to handle the situation so our little Julie would not be heartbroken or traumatized. We finally decided to tell her that we had to sell Bully. We just knew if we'd told her we had slaughtered the steer for food, she would never eat a bite of steak or hamburger again without wondering if it was Bully.

Julie carried on with her need to name the cattle, so next we had Bill Bailey. This was back before I had put up permanent fencing, relying only on the electric fence. Bill Bailey would be prone to ignoring the electric fencing and it seemed, every other day we were in the woods yelling "Bill Bailey, come home. Won't you come home, Bill Bailey? Won't you come home?"

Looking back, I realize that none of our cattle wanted to stay at home because the problem with the electric fence continued. One morning, I was running late leaving for the television station. Pulling out of the drive, I noticed the cows were out, but running late, all I could do was back the truck up and yell to Judy that the cows were out. Pre-cellphone days, of course. I couldn't stop to help, so I headed on to work.

When I got home that evening, Judy let me know she had had to run those cows all the way back to the barn. And just when she thought she was home free and they were at the barn, the cows bolted, as cows will do, and scattered to the four winds. She threw up her hands and told those cows "That's fine, you can go wherever you want. When Gene gets home. He can deal with you." She sounded just like she was talking to one of kids, "You just wait until your father gets home."

CHAPTER 4

TV GENE AND FARMER GENE

WGHP
If That Dog Bites Me…
The 100 Yard Dash
Gypsy
Hunter Chicken Farm
What Makes Your Garden Grow?
Dick Clark
The Duke Lives On
Chickies and Babies
Why Did the Chicken Cross The Road?
Buzzy Saves the Day
Bambi
Gene Hunter with Hair
Sunset Carson
President Nixon and Gerald Ford
Political Tongue and Cheek
Focus
Paul Harvey
The Chicken Farmer and the Chicken Peddler

WGHP

Just after beginning work at Channel 8, WGHP, the company hired a new General Manager, Phil Lombardo. He immediately began to implement numerous changes in our programming format. Currently, I was covering Raleigh's important events and anchoring the weekend news cast. Charlie Harville was on sports while also hosting Tuesday night wrestling; Jerry Merritt handled the weather and a morning show called Dialing for Dollars. Richard Buddine was the news anchor but left to anchor the news in another market. Phil called me in his office and offered me the news anchors job. My salary would almost double from what I was currently making as a reporter. I didn't make him wait more than ten seconds for my affirmative answer and I didn't let the door hit me in the rear on the way out. I was so excited, finally! I was off weekend work. The downside was that the job was second shift as it required two shows daily; The 5:30 and 11:00 evening news. I was also required to write and edit all of the copy. This required coordinating the film cuts with the photographer. Trust me, it made for a full day.

Gene Hunter Reports, At the anchor desk
Reprinted with permission from WGHP

Our operation was a little on the disorganized side. After taking the reins, I suggested we make some physical improvements. We needed to build a screening room, tear out some walls and doors. These were things that would greatly improve the flow of assimalating the newscast. Phil asked me to give him recommendations and said he didn't mind the cost if it accomplished the goal. I gave him a list of what needed to be done, what I thought it would cost and he called a contractor and got the quote.

A few days later Phil shared the estimate from the contractor with me. Since I was now free on weekends, I told him I would do it for half the price the contractor quoted as long as he would allow me to accomplish it in my own time. Phil questioned my experience, but after explaining that I had built my own home and completed several projects in the service for the major, I got the job. I loaded the tools in my 1960 El Camino, a real classic, and started that weekend. Phil opened an account with a building supply company that was close to the station to purchase materials as I needed them. I had some pretty nice paychecks for the next eight weeks since I was working seven days a week at the station.

Judy was glad when I finished the project and so was I. Most importantly, Phil was tickled with the results.

IF THAT DOG BITES ME...

Judy was at the farm alone with the kids until I arrived home after work. After some very quiet nights in the country, we decided we needed a guard dog for their safety. That was joyful words to the kid's ears as they had always wanted a dog. With my history with German Shepherds, we decided to try and find one. Judy saw an ad in the local paper for a "Free to good home German Shepherd". After I left for work that morning, she called, and arranged to see the dog immediately.

At first glance, the dog was a total disappointment. She was nothing but skin and bones and looked like she hadn't been fed in a month. But Judy looked into those gentle eyes and for whatever reason instantly connected with the dog. Judy said, "It was though the dog was saying, please get me out of here."

When Judy first arrived to look at the dog, she made the kids stay in the station wagon, unfamiliar dog and all. At first, the shepherd was very protective of its owner and didn't allow Judy to get very close. Judy took that as a good sign and went to the car to get some doggie treats she had brought along.

She spent forty-five minutes talking to the woman. Every few minutes, she would toss the dog some goodies. Gradually, he inched his way to her. Finally, he was close enough to take the last one from her hand. Judy rubbed the dog; the dog licked her hand and the bond was complete. Every human that met Judy loved her and animals were no different. The kids named the dog Baby.

It was around midnight when I came home that evening. I entered the kitchen off the side porch and heard a throaty growl as soon as I closed the door. Judy usually waited up for me but this time she was not alone having her new best friend, Baby, with her. Baby was having no part of a stranger coming in the house, especially this late at night. "Judy" I said, "If that dog bites me in my own house I'm gonna shoot it", of course, there may have been a few expletives in there. Judy just grinned, tossed me a couple of dog treats, and told me to give them to her slowly. Baby was a pushover for treats, good thing intruders didn't know that secret. She quickly adapted to the family. From the first night Judy brought her home, Baby slept in our bedroom, bedside the bed. We treated her for worms, and she started to put on weight. She finally topped out at around eight five pounds from the skinny fifty-pound pup Judy brought home.

Our house had a drive-in carport with a storm door entrance to the back porch leading into the kitchen. Normally during the day, Judy left the kitchen door open so Baby could lay on the porch in the sun but one day the door was closed, and Baby was in the house. Sometimes, the previous owner of the house would forget that he no longer owned the farm and would show up on occasion attempting to make himself right at home. When Judy heard the storm door open, she opened the kitchen door. Baby saw a strange man standing too close to her mama and lunged for his throat. Judy reacted quickly, grabbing at Baby's collar. It was pure luck that her small hand slid right in between the collar and Baby's fur as Baby was just inches from the man's throat. The man backed away quickly and was white as a sheet. He never attempted to enter the house again without calling first or knocking on the door. And I never had a need to worry about the family's safety as long as Baby was around.

During her breeding periods, we started tying Baby outside on a chain. One night, we woke to the howling of a dog in the far distance. Judy was adamant that it was Baby, and I was just as adamant that it was impossible because Baby was tied up under the carport. The dog kept howling and Judy kept nudging me. She said, "I know that's Baby, would you please go check on her". I could never refuse any of Judy's requests and it was obvious that I was not getting any sleep until I did as my wife asked. I put on my bathrobe, made my way through the house, turned on the carport light and voila', no Baby. She had somehow pulled the chain loose, and chain and all, had ran off. Judy was worried sick and informed me, yes informed me, I would have to go after her. It was two in the morning, we were surrounded by thousands of acres. But again, I could never refuse Judy's request and as much as I would like to sleep, knew I wouldn't get any until Baby was safely back at home. I did have the advantage of a full moon that night, so I strapped on my .45 caliber Army pistol and grabbed my service M1 carbine. I felt like I was back at Ramey and on horse patrol. With a high beam flashlight, I headed into the dark woods toward the sound. She continued to bark, making finding her a lot easier until I was a hundred yards into the woods, and she decided to be quiet. I called out to get her barking again. Another thirty yards into the woods I finally saw her. Baby's trailing chain had gotten wrapped around a dead, fallen tree, and she was struggling to get free. I didn't need any goodies that night to become her best friend. She was one happy camper to see me, licking me the entire time I was trying to free her. I gave some thought to asking her if the trip was worth it but changed my mind when I saw how elated she was to see me. It took a few minutes to get the chain unraveled from the fallen tree but when I did, I slung the carbine over my neck, used the chain as a leash and Baby and I headed home to the farm. Well I was headed for the farm, Baby kept trying to pull me in a different direction. I really thought she was "looking for a boyfriend", and I desperately wanted to go back to bed so I pulled her back toward the farm. I could see the outside lights of the house, so I knew we were headed home and getting close, but Baby was making it tough to stay on course.

We finally came out of the woods. But we were not at the farm. The beacon I followed home belonged to the neighbors, a quarter mile away from the farm. If I was smart, I would have just given Baby the lead and followed her home.

Baby ran away again. That last time, we were never able to locate her, nor did we ever find out exactly what happened to her. We like to think that someone picked her up and took her in. I realize that's highly unlikely given her demeanor toward strangers. But it would be the best outcome of any other scenario. She was one of the best guard dogs we ever had. Judy and the kids were heartbroken.

THE 100 YARD DASH

We raised German Shepherd puppies for a while. All three kids loved animals when they were small. But Julie loved every animal with her whole heart. And as you may very well guess, when the puppies came, Julie wanted to keep them all.

Shortly after losing Baby, we acquired another German Shepherd, Cookie. Cookie was one of only a few dogs not named Baby as Cookie was her registered name. Julie was six or seven and, as all little girls should be, spoiled rotten. When Julie didn't get her way, she would "run away from home." She was the youngest at the time, so I think I pampered her a little more than I should, and she came to expect it. She would always advise us of her impending journey and when she would head out, she would take our 120-pound German Shepherd with her along with a drink and a pack of nabs. Cookie would follow Julie everywhere. She would take Cookie by the leash and head up the road. She would make it to the edge of the property where an old cinder block building sat. And here I have to say, that my and your perspective of running away was a lot different than 7-year-old Julie. When Julie ran away from home, this is where she would go. She would sit in that building for a couple hours with Cookie until the sun started to set, then she would return home. We never had to worry about her, she was Cookies favorite family member. And no one, especially a stranger, would have been able to get close to her. God help the person who tried.

On average, Julie "ran away from home" about once a month. It could be more or less, depending on how often she didn't get her way. My little girl, being the creature of habit, always had the same routine. Always to the building, never more than 100 yards from home and always with Cookie. We finally convinced her that each time she ran away; she was leaving her Mama unprotected because she was taking Cookie with her. So, the 100-yard dashes came to a halt. That was, at least, until her teenage years.

Our family owned many horses through the years. Marcy had a gelding pony named Coco, named so for his chocolate color. He was a gentle pony, but a lazy pony. We had an old military jeep on the farm and everytime Marcy wanted to ride, I would tie Coco to the back of the jeep to exercise him first. Once you got him worn down a little, he was fine. He finally and eventually got over that exercise. If you've ever owned horses, you have to know that is not an uncommon trait with horses that go a while without being ridden.

Julie and Cookie, Kids on Horses

Often, the humor in a story is not fully realized at the time because of the tragedy surrounding it. Princess, our precious pony, had taught every kid that every visited to ride. Then one day, Princess fell ill. We had rented some pasture a little way up the road so I could install permanent fencing. We moved Princess and the rest of the horses to the rented pasture for a brief stay. Once they were moved, I divided a large stall in the barn into two smaller double stalls. It didn't take long to complete, but it was something I had wanted to do for some time. The partition consisted of a couple of two by fours and some one by fives, basically building a wooden wall. Having only 4 stalls had worked out so far as Tina and Princess always acted like mother and colt and we were able use the large stall for them. Now, all the horses would have their own stall.

Then I went to work on the fence. Our good friends John, a retired D.C. police officer, and his wife Leslie, came over to help. Leslie, could out work most men I knew. They brought their tractor to stretch the woven wire. We had a goal of completing five acres. I had figured it would take about a week to complete and had requested to use some of my vacation time. Boy, some vacation!

Hauling food and caring for our horses in the rented pasture fell to Judy and the kids. One evening after feeding, they came home and told me Princess was off her feed. We all jumped in the truck and went to the rented pasture. We tried everything, but couldn't get her to eat. Since we weren't with the horses at all times, we weren't even sure if she was drinking water. Fearing she was getting dehydrated, we haltered the pony and I slowly led Princess back to the farm and into the barn while Judy took the kids home in the pickup. We put her in her newly constructed stall, hoping being home would cure what ailed her, we gave her hay, a bucket of water as well as her normal portion of feed.

When I checked on her the next morning, she seemed to be better.

We finished the fence that week and when Monday rolled around, I headed back to work for my normal second shift. Judy rarely called me at work. She never wanted to burden me with trouble on the farm while I was working. And usually, if there was anything she couldn't handle, it could wait until I got home.

Judy took the kids to the barn to check on Princess. They found her lying on her side. Her feet were tangled under the partition I had constructed, and Princess wouldn't budge. Judy knew she had to get the pony on her feet. She sent Marcy to get a sledge hammer and while the kids kept Princess calm, Judy used all her might to demolish my newly constructed wall. There wasn't anything left that could even be reused. Funny how it only takes a few minutes to tear down what took a half day to build. I could see my petite little wife slinging that sledge hammer, wood flying everywhere, just to get that pony on his feet. And she was successful.

At the breakfast table the next morning, the kids were relaying the story to me. They explained how my little Wonder Woman, aka Miss Paul Bunyon had destroyed my fine carpentry work. We laughed all morning about that. After breakfast, I got my tools together and headed to the barn to see if I could salvage anything from Judy's handiwork. I got a scoop of feed to pour into Princesses bucket, but when I took it to her stall, I found her lying on the floor. She had passed away during the night from kidney failure. I have never been much of one to cry over animals, but I shed a tear or two over that sweet pony. She was family and she had been in the family for eight years. Princess hadn't just belonged to one person; she belonged to all of us and she was much loved by all.

Julie had ridden Princess for several years. While all of the kids were devastated, Julie was so heartbroken. I honestly thought we were going to have to bury her with the pony. I think the only thing that kept her going and got her through the loss of Princess was Cookie, the German Shepherd.

GYPSY

We decided she needed something to get her mind off Princess and the best thing was another horse. Although still heartbroken, she became excited about the new adventure as we headed off to the horse sale. We found a medium size mare with a light mane and tail. The horse was in rough shape; it had the mange, was so skinny her ribs showed and had an absessed frog in one foot causing it to be sore. I knew all these things could be straightened out in time and Julie liked her. She named her Gypsy before we even bought her. Julie was all about getting that horse healthy. I helped and showed her what had to be done. Everyday we mixed medication in Gypsy's feed and swabbed her coat with antiseptic. She was bathed a couple of times a week. I lanced her frog, draining the infection and soaking it in a bucket of warm water and hydrogen peroxide 30 minutes a day. My standard treatment with a new horse was to treat for worms. Julie was busy with Gypsy and didn't have time to mourn for Princess anymore. The transformation was incredible in them both. Within a month Gypsy was running in the pasture. Her lameness was gone, and she was kicking up her heels. Her coat was slick and shiny, and the mange had disappeared. She gained weight so you could no longer see her ribs. And the cough had totally disappeared. And Julie had found a new friend. Julie rode Gypsy for many years and the two bonded in an amazing way. When Julie would dismount (and she rode bareback as often as with a saddle) Gypsy would follow her and Cookie around the yard like a second puppie. Julie would stop, Gypsy would stop. It was truly an amazing connection between horse and rider as well as seeing both parties experience an emotional and physical cure.

HUNTER CHICKEN FARM

We had three gardens that grew the vegetables we would need to keep us going. We grew, picked, canned and froze most of the food our family would eat. We bought very few groceries other than the basics; salt, sugar, flour etc. During the summer months, we would fill our three freezers with vegetables, beef and chicken to carry us through the winter months.

Even with growing most of our food, we had come to the decision that for Judy to continue to remain at home with the kids, we would have to find some sort of supplemental income. Raising chickens would be our next step.

We borrowed $15000.00 on the farm and built a modern chicken house. It was 10,000 square feet (40 x 250) with a cinder block foundation, steel trusses, retractable curtains and heaters that were suspended from the roof. John Hutchins was a contractor, and a church friend. He had three chicken houses and helped us lay it out. Working second shift at the television station left most of the responsibility of tending to the chickens to Judy and the kids. With the chicken house completed, the feeders and feed in place, we received our contract from Cargill, a facility in Siler City. We began in the chicken business raising pullets. From chick to pullet took about six to eight weeks. Then they were off to market.

We were all excited on the day of their arrival. It was amazing to see seven thousand chickens in one place. The six-foot burners were on cables and could be lowered and raised as needed. Baby chicks had to be kept warm with the gas heaters, so we built a cardboard fence around each burner about eight foot in diameter. The chicks came in cardboard containers of a hundred to the container and we were able to put seven boxes or 700 chicks around each burner. While they were in the temporary fencing, we had to fill their waterers and feeders by hand. Until they became big enough to eat from the automatic waterer and feeder that circled the entire interior of the house. Once they reached that stage, we took down their temporary fencing. For the first few weeks, as with any baby, we took turns getting up in the middle of the night to check on them. Even though the chicken house was secure, and the flourescent lights were always on at night, there was still the danger of weasels or snakes eating them. When chickens become frightened, they will head in droves to the nearest corner and with large quantities of chickens, this can cause some chickens to get smothered to death. Since our contract was based on the number of chickens we delivered, Judy was very concientious about caring for them and we lost very few, even though, sometimes its impossible to prevent.

Everything in the chicken house was automated. There was a switch controling the auger which dumped the feed from the bin to the holding tank inside the chicken house. The feeder would disperse about 200-300 pounds of feed at a time and it had to be filled up daily. At some point during the day, the power had gone off and one of the kids hadn't realized they'd left the switch for the auger in the on position. This happened just before Cargill delivered the feed. Judy was in the house and heard the truck fill the bin. She was busy sewing, canning, or cooking but when she heard the clanging from the chicken house, she went to check on all the noise. When she opened the door to the wire enclosed feeder room, she was confronted with 3 tons of feed from floor to ceiling. Judy, in her normal calm, collected, self, waded through the feed, flipped off the auger switch and walked calmly back to the house. She called Cargill, and politely explained what happened. They sent a truck immediately to suck all the feed out of the feeder room of the chicken house and pump it back into the bin. The walls of the feeder room were wire, protecting the chickens from getting crushed by the food but the wire allowed a lot of food to fall into the chicken house. Those chickens were fed well that day. Judy's calm and collected response, was "there was nothing I could do about it, so why worry about it".

About the same time, we lost Julie's favorite companion, the German Shepherd Cookie. We had a garbage collection service. The cans were located behind the house, leaving the collection service to drive down our driveway to empty the cans. As the garbage man was headed out the driveway, Cookie, protecting her property, got too close to the wheels of the garbage truck and was struck and killed. The whole family was devastated as we held a funeral for Cookie. We cancelled the garbage collection service after that and started burning our trash in two fifty-five gallon drums.

WHAT MAKES YOUR GARDEN GROW?

Chicken house

Earlier in the century, in the southern part of the county where we lived, the electricity was often sporadic. Many times, it would go out when it seemed the most critical time. We had a seperate faucette on the wall next to the cooler room and an excellent well that supplied water to our home and the chicken house. The pump running the well requires electricity to move the water from the well to the holding tank. One Friday, Judy sent Marcy to the chicken house to turn on the faucette and run water to the

7000 chickens (on cold nights in the winter, we had to cut off the water to the automatic waterers to keep them from freezing). When Marcy turned on the faucette, the power was out so there was no water. Judy immediately called the power company as power was critical to operate the automated track that carried the feed and then sent Marcy, Julie and Russ on to school. About an hour later the power came on. Judy went to check on the automatic feeder and make sure the timer was set properly after the outage. She opened the walk-in door at the end of the house and stepped in a puddle of water. When Marcy attempted to give the chickens water, she forgot to turn the faucette off. About a third of the ten-thousand-foot chicken house was flooded. Judy waded over to the faucette and cut it off.

I was working in High Point, but this was an emergency and I had to leave work. We stood a chance of losing the entire flock if we did not act quickly. When too much moisture is in a house, it can spread rapidly, and infect the entire flock. It was noon by the time I got home after a forty-five-minute drive. The situation was so dire, Judy had picked the kids up from school. Marcy was very upset when told about it, but it was a mistake and could have as easily been made by a grownup. We were not placing blame, we were focused on fixing the problem.

All the chickens were herded to the clean and dry portion of the chicken house. We quickly erected a temporary wall to keep them securely in that area allowing us to open the two large double doors at the end of the building. We had no tractor, so there was no loader, just me, Judy, three kids and a pickup truck. We all grabbed a shovel and started to work. Poor Marcy worked the hardest, I guess she felt responsible for it all. We shoveled and hauled off between twelve and fourteen pickup loads of wet manure. The chicken house was cleaned all the way to the dirt floor. We finished around midnight, stopping only to eat a bite. Once the chicken house was clean and dry, we had to order a dump truck full of fresh shavings, lime the floor to expedite the drying process and spread out the new load of shavings over the clean area. After finishing the monumental task, we removed the temporary wall to allow the chickens back into the area. We were totally exhausted, but I don't think we lost a single bird. I was so proud of the kids. And we had a heck of a garden that year with all the nitrogen in the manure.

DICK CLARK

His real name is Richard Augustus Wagstaff, but you know him better as Dick Clark. Anyone in America who has ever watched American Bandstand is very familiar with him. He is the kid who never aged. I'm not exactly sure if he created Dick Clark Productions before or after American Bandstand, but in 1968, his company was shooting a movie in Ramseur, North Carolina. I had never been on location during the filming of a picture, so this was a new experience for me. I gotta tell you, it was actually very boring. They do more sitting around waiting or getting ready for their shots than they do actual work. For those thinking acting is a pie job, we were on location 12 hours and they only filmed 5 minutes of a 90-minute film.

Movie people are not fools and welcome with open arms, any media that affords them free publicity. They were filming *Killers III*, starring Dick Clark along with the up and coming young star, Robert Walker. Walker was never a big star but did have thirty-five movies to his credit. He played opposite Burt Lancaster and Joanne Dru in the western *Vengence Valley*. Walker was also the drunken ordinance man in *The War Wagon* with John Wayne and Kirk Douglas. One of Walkers more memorable roles was as music composer, Jerome Kern in "Till The Clouds Roll By". Kern was known for writing *Showboat* starring North Carolina native Ava Gardner.

When the noon break came, the entire cast and crew sat down to a long row of picnic tables. Since I was interviewing Dick Clark about the movie, we sat across the table from him. It was a working lunch. Dick was a most pleasant host and had that star quality about him. While we ate catered fried chicken and trimmings, we discussed the production of *Killers III*. The overpowering star magnitude of Dick Clark filming in the Tar Heel

State was more of a story than the movie. Dick Clark Productions made about fifteen movies, but his true fame came from American Bandstand.

I was not as excited about seeing Dick Clark as most young people would have been. Now John Wayne would have been a totally different story. I would have paid the television station for that privilege. But Dick Clark still looks good on a resume'.

THE DUKE LIVES ON

Since most of you know the household name of Johns Wayne aka "The Duke" Morrison, you will better understand this story. This happened just prior to the Duke's death. Robert Scheuller's daughter Cindy, was in a motorcycle accident and had to have one of her legs amputated. Wayne heard Robert Scheuller tell her story on one of his *Hour of Power* broadcasts and being a fan of Scheullers, he wrote a letter to Cindy in the hospital. Wayne had a reputation for constantly answering fan mail to all of his fans, even the younger ones. He wrote "Dear Cindy. Sorry to hear about your accident. Hope you will be alright. Signed John Wayne."

When she got the letter, she decided she wanted to write the Duke a reply. "Dear Mr. Wayne, I got your note. Thanks for writing to me. I like you very much. I am going to be all right because Jesus is going to help me. Mr. Wayne, do you know Jesus? I sure hope so because I can't imagine heaven being complete without John Wayne being there. I hope if you don't know Jesus that you will give him your heart right now. See you in heaven" and she signed her name.

She had just signed her name and wrote John Wayne on the envelope when a visitor came in the room to see her and asked, "What are you doing?" She said "I just wrote a letter to John Wayne, but I don't know how to get it to him." To which he replied that he was having dinner with John Wayne that night at the Newport Club in Newport Beach. "Give it to me and I'll give it to him". She gave him the letter and he put it in his coat pocket.

That night there were twelve men sitting around and cutting up when the guy happened to reach in his pocket and felt the letter. John Wayne was seated at the end of the table, so the guy passed it down and John Wayne opened it. They kept on laughing and cutting up when someone happened to look down at John Wayne to see that he was crying. One of them said

"Hey Duke, what's the matter". He said, "I want to read you this letter". He read the letter and then began to weep. He folded the letter, put it in his pocket, and pointed to the man who delivered it to him and said "You go tell that little girl right now, in this restaurant, right here, John Wayne gives his heart to Jesus Christ and I will see her in heaven." Three weeks later John Wayne died.

From one cowboy to another, I'm looking forward to meeting you Duke.

CHICKIES AND BABIES

From the beginning of our marriage, Judy and I wanted more children. And finally, in 1968, we found out we were expecting. Unfortunately, this was not meant to be and Judy and I lost our son when she miscarried. We were devastated.

The devastation quickly turned to elation when Judy found out she was pregnant again right away. And in the August of 1969, we were blessed with the birth of our fourth child, Michael. Michael was born with a knee disfigurement, so the doctor put him in a cast for several months. Boy was that fun? Everytime you would change his diaper, he would kick you with his cast. But the pain was worth it and when the cast came off, Michael had no lingering problems.

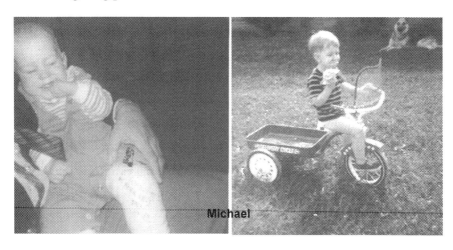

Michael

Michael was six months old when we decided to go from raising pullets into the layer business producing eggs. We changed companies and put in metal nests. We installed a refrigeration room to store the eggs until they were picked up and a sliding rail cart system to transport the eggs from one end of the chicken house to the other and then to the refrigeration room.

I had not had time to completely finish the installation of the track. It was lacking the last six feet from the refrigeration room. It was usable, you just had to remember to stop the cart before it got to the end of the track. If you didn't, it looked something like a train derailment. Judy and the kids knew this and knowing how busy I was didn't complain about the situation, they just stopped the cart before the end. The cart held about sixty dozen eggs at a time. Judy was a stay at home mom that cared for 4 kids, 4 horses, a dog and God only knows how many chickens. So, sometimes, she had other things on her mind during her collection rounds. One day, on her final trip back to the cooler, she forgot about the unfinished track and gave the cart a big push. It went right off the end of the track. Seven hundred eggs lay on the ground in a giant egg souffle. Well if you know anything about chickens, you know they will eat anything. Even their own eggs. They had a chick fest, no pun intended. Judy salvaged what wasn't broken, washed them off and put them in the cooler. One thing is for sure, I found time to finish that track when I got home that evening. It's incredible that a person can find time to finish a chore after an eggtastrophy like that.

Judy installed a small television in the isolation room so Michael would be entertained watching television while she made her morning rounds collecting the eggs. Occasionally when the wind was blowing through the chicken house, Judy would sit Michael in his seat and let him ride on the egg cart. It was like in a stroller as it rolled along the track and he giggled and cooed and seemed to thoroughly enjoy it. The egg cart had two levels, a top shelf and a bottom shelf. We had this one chicken that had moulted, so he was as bald....well, as bald as I am now. The three olders kids named the chicken just that, Baldie. Well that bald chicken would perch on the cart next to Michael. He was close enough for Michael to touch, and Michael would rub and pet him and coo and giggle some more. Chickens love pecking at shiny objects and Baldie was no different. Well, Michael was in his seat, petting Baldie when Baldie looked Michael in the eyes, his shiny blue eyes. And pretty as you please, Baldie reached over and pecked Michael right in the eye. His eye was blood red for a week or two, but finally cleared up, fortunately with no lasting issues. The same can not be said for Baldie. The family had fried chicken for supper the next night, chicken that didn't even have to be plucked… pay back is hell.

Egg collection was twice a day; Judy normally handled the morning collection and the kids pulled the second pickup as soon as they got home after school. The kids were amazingly dependable in their collection. A normal day consisted of collecting 120 dozen eggs. Then, the contracting company picked up the collected eggs a couple times a week.

When I was off work, I would help Judy or the kids with their rounds. The nests were back to back in rows so to collect, one person went down one side and another person went down the other side. They were off the ground about four feet, but you could see the person opposite you. Russ was collecting opposite me while the girls were going down the other row. Russ was seven. He always wore this flat top hair cut, that reminded me of a landing field. During the collection, a chicken laid an egg in my hand. Freshly laid eggs are rubbery until they hit the air. At which point, they harden almost instantly. It was just of those moments that the devil made me do. I gently lobbed the egg across the nest and made a perfect three-point landing on the top of Russ's head. Russ looked up, egg slowly making its way down his forehead and uttered the worst thing he knew at that age, "Daddy, you're SELFISH!" and took off to the house bawling to tell his mama.

I paid the price because I had to collect all my eggs and Russ's too. Julie and Marcy laughed through the rest of their row. I apologized to him later in the only way a dad can truly apologize to a kid that age, I took him for some ice cream.

WHY DID THE CHICKEN CROSS THE ROAD

Let's ask the age-old question "Why did the chicken cross the road". Now to most of you, the obvious answer would be to get to the other side. But that's not the answer from well-known and prominent figures in various celebrity fields. Here are some of their answers.

George W. Bush-We don't really care why the chicken crossed the road. We just want to know if the chicken is on the other side or not. This chicken is either for us or against us. There's no middle ground here.

Al Gore-I invented the chicken. I invented the road. Therefore, the chicken crossing the road represented the application of these two different functions of government in a new reinvented way to bring greater services to the american people.

Pat Buchanan-To steal a job from a decent, hardworking American.

Rush Limbaugh-I don't know why the chicken crossed the road, but I'll bet it was getting a government grant to cross the road. I bet right now someone is forming a support group to help chickens with crossing the road syndrome. Chickens crossing roads paid for by tax dollars and I am talking about your money, money the government took from you to build roads for the chicken to cross.

Martha Stewart-No one called to warn me which way that chicken was going. I had a standing order at the farmers market to sell my eggs when the price dropped to a certain level. No little bird gave me any inside information.

Dr. Seuss-Did the chicken cross the road? Did he cross it with a toad? Yes, the chicken crossed the road, but why it crossed I've not been told.

Ernest Hemingway-To die. In the rain. Alone.

Martin Luther King Jr.-I envision a world where all chickens will be free to cross roads without having their motives called into question.

Albert Einstein-Did the chicken really cross the road or did the road move beneath the chicken.

Bill Clinton-I did not cross the road with that chicken. What do you mean by chicken? Define chicken please?

Aristotle-It is the nature of chickens to cross the road.

Captain Kirk-To boldly go where no chicken has gone before.

Colonel Sanders-I missed one

BUZZY SAVES THE DAY

Marcy, Russ and Julie would saddle up Coco, Amigo and Gypsy every day after they completed their chores. I was raising a house full of cowboys and cowgirls. They would ride all over that seventy acres. Normal days would bring them back home just before dark, the curfew for country kids. During their rides, they had one favorite spot that I knew about. They would pack a lunch and head out. When they reached their spot, they would unsaddle their horses, lay on their backs, eat their lunches and talk for hours.

Once they became really good in the saddle, they started a Christmas tradition. They would head into the woods and cut down our Christmas Tree. Then they would form a triangle, tie the tree to ropes and the ropes to the saddle horns and haul the tree back to the house. Even as adults, during the Christmas season, they still talked of those Christmas's they brought home the Christmas tree.

When Michael was several years old and could maintain his balance, we would let him ride with Marcy on Sugar. One day they were riding close to the house and Marcy left Michael sitting on Sugar to run in the house for a glass of water. Sugar was ground broke, meaning if the reins were dangling, she would stand. However, Marcy left the reins on the saddle horn with Michael sitting in the saddle. While Marcy was in the house, Sugar decided she was ready to go to the barn, or maybe Michael thought he was old enough to ride to the barn by himself. We still aren't sure exactly what part Michael played in all of this. He could have urged her to giddyup. But for some reason, Sugar headed to the barn at a dead run. The barn was down a hill, across a creek and up another hill. Russ on his horse, Amigo, saw what was happening and being the protective big brother, immediately gave chase. When Russ took off, Julie was on Gypsy, and for whatever reason, dismounted. Gypsy had a bad habit of turning in circles when you tried to mount her. Julie tried to get back on Gypsy, but Gypsy just continued to turn in circles. Julie told the horse, "Please Gypsy, if you're ever going to stand still, stand still now". Gypsy must have sensed the tense situation, because the horse stopped moving immediately and stood completely still letting Julie mount quickly and take chase after Russ. All this occurred in the bat of an eye, literally only a matter of seconds. By the time Russ caught up with Sugar, Sugar was at the barn standing still. The cinch was not tight, and during the run to the barn the saddle had slowly slid to Sugar's side. Michael was hanging on for dear life. Russ, still in the saddle, reached over and grabbed Michael by the collar. Michael, a little shook up after his sideways ride, looked up at Russ and said, "Thank you Buzzy, you saved me." Julie arrived at the barn and Marcy walked out of the house just as Russ was grabbing Michael. Marcy never again left Michael alone on a horse. Looking back, its a wonder we didn't have more broken bones than we did. The lord does watch over fools and children.

In those days, the kids were always putting on pretend horse shows and asking me to be the judge, albeit a trap I did not want to fall into. I was very careful to make sure they all won. One for best dressed, one for cleanest, one for anything I could think of at the time. No one left the Hunter Chicken House Horse Show a loser. I may have been born at night, but I wasn't born last night.

BAMBI

While at Channel Eight, I covered a story in Winston Salem's Tanglewood Park. They were thinning out the deer population that roamed through the wooded areas because of the danger to tourists. I introduced myself to the Park Manager, covered the story and interviewed him. I inquired as to how they disposed of the deer and he informed me they would be tranquilized and shipped to the Uwharrie National Forest near Asheboro to be freed. Some of the deer were small fawn and still had their baby spots. After the interview, I told him about my farm and asked him if I could have one of the fawns. I thought the kids would get a kick out of having a deer at the farm and it would be a learning experience for all of us. He agreed as long as I was willing to transport it. We came up with the time for pickup the next day, finished our story and left. The next day, I rented an enclosed cargo trailer and drove the sixty miles to Tanglewood. When I got there, the manager met me as promised, found a fawn and proceeded to shoot it with the tranquilizer gun. The fawn was small, so in a matter of minutes he was out of it. I picked up his limp body, layed him on hay I had put in the trailer, thanked the manager and headed home. I was about ten miles from the house when the trailer started banging around like it had a flat. I pulled off on the side of a rural country road. The sedation had worn worn off and the fawn was bouncing off the walls of the trailer. I'm sure between pitch darkness inside of the trailer and the movement of the vehicle the poor thing was scared to death. I couldn't risk opening the doors to check on him because if he bolted past me it would have been Saturday Night in Dodge City. I got back in the pickup and proceeded to the house. He finally settled down some but continued to make enough noise that I knew he was still alive.

When I drove past the house, I honked the horn so Judy and the kids, all excited about the new addition, could ride with me to the barn. The barn had a wide hallway, so I backed the trailer right up to an empty stall and released him. We gave him plenty of hay and water and left him for the night to settle down and adjust to his new surroundings. I gave strict instructions to the kids not to let him out or they would never see him again. We kept him stalled up for about four weeks. During that time, the kids gave him apples and other goodies and at the end of that time, we had a pet deer, Bambi. They were rubbing him and he was following them around like they were his mother and he was their puppy.

I told them we needed to release him into the pasture with the horses. After being cooped up for so long he was so full of energy, he was vaulting six feet in the air spooking the horses. It was a circus for a while until they finished the perfomance.

It didn't take long for the horses to settle down then the fawn settled down and everybody went back to grazing. He stayed in the pasture, bonding with the horses for months, and would come to the kids for treats just like always. I guess as he grew older his wild instincts got the better of him because late in the evening, he would jump the fence and head for the woods. But the next morning at sunrise, he was right back grazing with the horses. This went on until he had grown his first set of antlers and was probably rutting and looking for a mate –the call of the wild. Then one day he just mysteriously disappeared, and we never saw him again. There was an article in the local newspaper shortly after Bambi disappeared where a farmer in our area had wrestled a deer to the ground. We never knew for sure but was always suspicious that it may be Bambi. I mean how many deer have you seen that you could get close enough to wrestle to the ground. I mean c'mon.

GENE HUNTER WITH HAIR

The lights in the television studio were not like the flourescent lights of today. The huge cone shaped lamps hanging from the ceiling would generate a lot of heat. It was non uncommom to start sweating within a few minutes of going on the air. The lights were hot and they were bright. My sandy blonde hair was thinning after years of wearing a tight military hat coupled with hereditary traits. The lights reflecting off my glistening scalp made my hair look even thinner. Phil Lambardo, the station manager, called me in his office one day and said "Gene, I'll make you a deal. I'll send off to New York and order you a partial toupee' if you agree to wear it." Well, the show must go on, so I agreed. He didn't skimp and when it got to North Carolina, Phil hired a barber to come to the studio for a fitting. He pulled my sandy colored hair back and shaved about a three-inch circle just above my forehead. He put two-sided tape on the toupee' and stuck it to the freshly shaved spot on my head. Then he proceeded to pull my own hair back and skillfully weave it into the toupee'.

We were on a deadline for the 5:30 news so there was no time for the barber to thin everything out and make it look natural. That was going to have to wait until the next day. I went on the air as scheduled at 5:30 and anchored the news. When I got home that night, the kids were trying to figure out who was kissing their mama. The next day one of the girls in accounting told me she had just walked in the door when the news came on at home. Her husband leaned back in his chair said "Look honey, they've got a new anchorman on Channel Eight". "Naw" she said, "that's just Gene Hunter with hair". I went to the barber the next morning to get it cut and thinned out. The next newscast, it was the same ole Gene Hunter.

Farmer Gene and television personality toupee' Gene was a tough mix. I had to change the two-sided tape almost every day. Trying to complete my daily chores at the farm meant some days I didn't leave for work as early as I should and on those days I didn't always have time to change the tape on my toupee. When I went on the air, the sweat from the hot lights in the studio loosened the old tape. While I was reading the news script, I could feel the toupee' slowly moving down my forehead. It was becoming very distracting to me. My director thought I was nuts when I cued the commercial two stories ahead of time. Directors never like surprises, it messes up their feeling of being in control. He could see in the off-air monitor that I was feverishly working to press the toupee' back on my head in hopes that it would make it through the rest of the show. I don't think it moved enough for the audience to see, but I never went on the air again without fresh tape.

SUNSET CARSON

While I was still a reporter at WGHP-TV in High Point, I was assigned to cover the show that Sunset Carson was putting on at the Carolina Theatre in Greensboro. Wow! To a cowboy that was a dream come true. I readied myself for the interview by doing a lot of research on Sunset before the show. Carson was born November 12, 1927 in Plainview, Texas. By the age of 12, he had competed in over 40 rodeos. He won every riding contest possible; bronc busting, bulldogging, calf roping and trickriding. Carson was once invited to join Tom Mix on his show which he did for a short while. He later went to South America to compete against the Vaqqueros, some of the world's finest cowboys. He was so good that in 1941 and 1942, he became South Americas All Around Champion Cowboy. Don't let the Hollywood persona mislead you; he was all cowboy-the real McCoy.

Sunset Carson returned to the states and enlisted in the service. Following his time in service, he was cast in parts with Hopalong Cassidy. His big break came when Republic Pictures snatched him up for what would become some of the best action westerns ever made. Sunset was a crack shot with both rifle and pistol and had quite a scenario in his show.

Being on the news staff, I was allowed back stage for an up close and personal. I took Michael with me. He was five or six at the time and his very existence had been threatened if he misbehaved. Sunset, whose real name was Michael Harrison, got his stage name when a director looked out his office window and saw a billboard that read Sunset Cars. It clicked and from then on, he was known as Sunset Carson.

My research on Sunset Carson paid off. He seemed very impressed with my knowledge of his background. He invited me and Michael to have lunch with him. Off we go. Sunset Carson was six foot six, wearing boots, spurs and double holstered six guns. And then there was me and Michael. Michael was on his best behavior, enthralled by this huge cowboy. Sunset has performed for the King and Queen of Siam. His fan clubs around the world numbered in excess of twenty million. He had made thirty pictures to date. Michael and I had a reason to strut. And he even bought our lunch. I wished many times that I kept the ticket from the meal. Sunset Carson and I connected that day. I would get a call from him from time to time just to say hello and see how I was doing.

After a lengthy lunch, we headed back across the street to the theatre. Once there, we were informed that the City Council refused to let Sunset Carson perform his show. It seems there is a city ordinance against discharging firearms inside the city limits. His whole show was built around his shooting exhibition. Sunset was loyal to his fans, and he knew they were going to be sorely disappointed. He contacted the city council in an attempt to appeal their decision, but they refused to make an exception. Since he was the star, he knew the show must go on. Sunset performed rope tricks, told stories and invited some of the kids on stage to show them how to twirl a rope. He confided in me later that it was one of his most enjoyable performances.

The Greensboro Daily News reported the story on Sunset Carson's show. After his performance, he presented the city council with a black hat, the symbol for the bad guys in the old west. They accepted it in good humor. Sunset Carson had the final say on that matter.

PRESIDENT NIXON AND GERALD FORD

In my teens, I had no interest in politics. Later in my life, I became totally immersed in it. My mother and the rest of her family were hard-core Republicans and when I turned eighteen, she urged me to register as a Republican. I did but didn't exercise my right to vote for quite a few years. Much to her chagrin, I have never voted a straight party ticket. I've never been one to believe that one party has all the right ideas. Over the years, I have become good friends with democrats and I'm even more convinced that a straight party ticket is the countrys nemesis.

Being the party faithful, Mom worked the elections and enjoyed all the social functions that went along with them. You can imagine her delight when Presidential Candidate Richard Nixon came to Burlington in 1968. You can imgine her further glee in having her picture taken with him at the Burlington Armory. While here, he also made an appearance at the Williams High Football Stadium. The picture shows Nixon in the background with an obvious Secret Service Agent staring at the camera. You don't have to have good vision to spot these guys because they are the ones never looking at the candidate, but instead, at all those who are looking at the candidate. Mom was very impressed with Nixon, but he ended up letting her down just like he did so many other Americans.

Nixon with Mom, Nixon visiting Williams High

I remember Lyndon Johnson said, "Jerry Ford was a nice guy, but he played too much football without his helmet". In redneck terms, he was short a few bricks from having a whole stack. You have to consider the source.

After the 37th President of the United States resigned, Vice President Gerald Ford was sworn in as POTUS. Being a benevolent man, he promptly pardoned his former boss. My mind quickly flashed back to the time I was assigned to cover Gerald Ford in a speech he was giving at Duke University. He was a congressman then and when I first entered the room, he crossed to meet me with an outstretched hand and the ever-present politician smile. In all my coverage of famous people, they all seem to have a stoic demeanor about them, like they know something the rest of us don't. Gerald Ford was no different. As we sat down for the interview he commented with a slight grin "Now go easy on me, ok?" I was thinking, "Sure, right". We had a very friendly interview, little did I realize at that moment, I was interviewing the next President of The United States, the first Chief Executive to reach the white house without being elected. He was just another political public servant; which reporters generally hate to cover. Give me fires, bank robberies, murders, anything except trying to make a politician into a headline story. Remember what I said about movie people? Politicians are the same, free press and lots of publicity; they never stop craving it. I am a very amiable person with an affable smile, so we hit it off. He was dressed to the nines, every hair in place, shoes so slick you could ice skate on them and what I imagine was one of my fraternity brother Bill Wallaces Hickey Freeman suits.

I do not remember what topic we were supposed to be addressing, because with his football experience and Delta Kapa Epsilon Fraternal backgroiund, we talked about everything except what I was assigned to cover. Finally, my cameraman had to break up the party. He reminded me we had to get the film to the station in time for processing before air time.

During parts of that interview, I remember talking about war. I told him about my father and his death on Iwo Jima. Ford was a commissioned officer. He attained Liuetenant Commander on the USS Monterey, an aircraft carrier. He saw action in ten battles as the Monterey took part in the armada's Island Hopping Campaign toward Japan. I guess knowing my father was on one of the ships didn't damage the interview process by any means. I can be a politician too sometimes.

Gerald or Jerry as he insisted I call him, seemed to have so much charisma about him. And I was calling the future President by his first name. I made the remark to John on the way back to the station that I sensed for some odd reason, that I had just shaken hands with greatness. I had occasion to call him in later years when I needed information on stories. He always remembered me and was very gracious in helping me. Don't be disillusioned by that statement—all politicians are more than well versed in how to manipulate the news media. Never for once did I ever deceive myself into thinking otherwise

Sam Ervin

United States Senator
from North Carolina
In office
June 5, 1954 – December 31, 1974
Preceded by   Clyde R. Hoey
Succeeded by Robert B. Morgan

Sam Ervin

After Ford became President, I would interview the man responsible for putting him in the White House. A democrat, Senator Sam Ervin of North Carolina, was on the committee that brought down Senator Joe McCarthy in 1954. He was head of the infamoius Watergate Commiittee that led to President Nixons resignation. His home was in Raleigh and on one of his trips back to North Carolina, we arranged an interview with him. That was a long time ago but I'm sure it pertained to Watergate and I'm sure we got absolutely nothing of any real news value out of it.

John, my cameraman and I were always up to something mischievous. Often just to make the assignment a little more palatable. We really had fun after the Senator left. John and I did a quick cutaway of me. When we got back to the station and processed the film, we took part of the footage with the Senator and edited it into my cutaway. It showed me asking the senator a question, and the senator answered the question. The cutaway was of me saying "No s—-, Senator, did he really say that". Of course, it never aired and was just for our amusement. The news crew cracked up. I still have the footage on DVD and, to me, its just as funny now as it was then.

POLITICAL TONGUE AND CHEEK

A few years back prior to one of the elections, I wrote a little tongue in cheek article, maybe more tongue than cheek, about the job requirements for President of the United States. Based on some of the Presidents that have been elected they fill the requirements easily enough.

1. Be able to articulate but have no common sense.
2. Be religiously affiliated but have no morals.
3. Have the ability to spend money but not necessary to be able to balance a checkbook.
4. Must be a control freak with unstable characteristics
5. Secret desire to be a rock star or movie star
6. No clue as to why the 2nd amendment was written.
7. Must be totally unaware of the powers of the constitution
8. Cannot have any compassion for senior citizens
9. Must be distantly related to Napoleon
10. Must have read and memorized Hitlers Mein Kempf
11. Cannot have read about or understood any American History
12. Must be able to reverse position instantly on any political issue making it sound like it was their original position.
13. Be reasonably proficient at a McDonalds drive thru

FOCUS

While at Channel Eight, I did a Sunday afternoon talk show "Focus", a news show with high profile people. The list of people was endless, but some really stood out.

On numerous occasions, I interviewed High Point Police Chief Laurie Pritchard. The High Point beat was dominated by Channel Eights Bobbie Martin, a dedicated journalist with no concern for the time involved in getting a story. She gained the confidence of the chief and would ride with him on serious news events. Chief Pritchard was nationally renowned as the Chief that jailed Martin Luther King Jr. during the sit-in protests in Selma, Alabama. He was a stocky red head, who lifted weights regularly, and carried a chrome plated pearl handle .38 pistol. Bobbi had the front row seat on this story and she told the news staff parts of it that never aired.

The black community was having a peaceful demonstration in High Point. Members from the Salisbury Ku Klux Klan were coming in to stir up trouble. Pritchard and Bobbi staked out one end of Main Street while another officer staked out the other end. As marchers were starting their parade, Pritchard spotted the car his informant had told him about. There were three men in the front seat and three in the back seat. With his lights blinking, he tapped his siren for a second and pulled the car over to the curb. The other officer had been informed of the stop and had pulled up in front of the men. The chief slowly walked to the driver's side of the vehicle. The other officer stood directly in its path. Bobbi was within ear shot of it all. They rolled their window down and Pritchard introduced himself as the Police Chief of High Point. He asked them where they were headed. The driver told them into High Point, to which the chief replied "I don't think that's a good idea tonight ". The driver started giving the chief some attitude about his rights. Pritchard, being a southern Alabama boy, pulled his chrome plated pistol, cocked the hammer and laid it on the driver's door. In his slow southern drawl, he exclaimed to the driver "If you move this vehicle one inch closer to my town, I will blow you to hell just as sure as grits is groceries." The car made a rapid u-turn and sped out of town. The news department did not include this in the report. Knowing the chief as I had come to, theres no doubt those gentlemen made a wise choice that night.

PAUL HARVEY

We had a two-minute insert with Paul Harvey every night. When he visited our studios, I got the opportunity to interview him for Focus. The station occupied the second and third floors of a downtown hotel and had one room set up for interviews.

Paul was traveling around the country to promote his syndicated news inserts and already famous radio style. He was a big hit on radio, but few people had ever seen him in person. As Paul got off the elevator, I introduced myself and shook his hand. He must have sensed my anxiety, because he immediately made a remark that put me at ease. He was much at home in broadcasters' surroundings which served for a much more relaxed interview.

Paul was dressed in a sharkskin suit and was immaculate in his attire from head to foot. Our General Manager was a dapper dresser, but when the two met, it was no contest.

The Promotion Department sat in on the interview and took pictures of us for publicity. This was Paul Harvey, nationally known on 600 radio stations. While this was his first adventure in television, he wasn't taking too much of a risk. He was already a household name.

I learned Paul wrote all his own copy. Even when it became too large a task for him, he still maintained editing rights over anything he verbalized.

Paul Harvey had a unique delivery in his broadcasts unlike any I have seen or heard. Much of it came from years of experience in life. He was indeed a unique master of his craft.

THE CHICKEN FARMER AND
THE CHICKEN PEDDLER

Another celebrity I interviewed on Focus was Colonel Harlan Sanders. Have you ever noticed that everybody from the south held the rank of Colonel? I guess the Colonels made up the fighting force and left the privates to command. Colonel Sanders started his famous chicken receipe late in life. He was around sixty-eight when I interviewed him. He didn't start peddling his chicken until he was sixty-five years old. He was a true southern gentleman with a walking cane, white hat, suit and shoes. He was easy to spot and would stand out in a crowd from three blocks away. I don't remember much about the interview. But I was a chicken farmer and he was a chicken peddler. He became a millionaire overnight, but money was not what it was all about. He just wanted to share his delicious recipe consisting of eleven herbs and spices. The Wall Street geniuses that bought his franchise and took it worldwide are still making billions. They are the same tycoons that own Taco Bell and Burger King.

Robert Morgan from Lillington was an old friend and former State Representative. He was on the show frequently., He continued his appearances as a State Attorney General and one-term U.S. Senator. He told me that Washington was a little too much politics for him. When he was in the State House, we would occassionally have lunch together. Our usual hangout was Pizza Hut. He was just a good old country boy who didn't believe in "getting above his raising". Bob passed away several years back from lingering problems of a brain tumor.

There were several other governors on the show over the years, along with other famous dignitaries.

The children were growing. And, as children grow, the expenses of the household grow as well. I loved being in broadcast news, but as a provider had to make choices that were the best for my family. I left the occupation I loved for the family I loved more.

CHAPTER 5

THE REST OF MY STORY

The Greatest Show on Earth
A Cowboy's Prayer
Judy – Career Woman
The Salesman
And We Traveled
Jenny
My Little Runaway
Who Shot JR?
Hee Haw
Freemasons
Did She Rob the Bank?
My Paso Finos
No Comb-Overs in the Pool
The QVC Queen
Ring the Dinner Bell
The Horse Belonged to Who?
Cowboys Love Their Peach Cobbler
Cowboys with Computers
Learning a New Language
News Events that Affected My Life
The Home Stretch

THE GREATEST SHOW ON EARTH

This story occurred several years after I left broadcasting. I know it was after I left because as the good ole' boys would say, had I still been in broadcasting, I would have been smack dab in the middle of it.

You woudn't know who I was talking about if I said this story is about Leonard Franklin Slye or David Weston from Cinncinnati, Ohio, but you will undoubtedly know the name Roy Rogers. Yep the real deal, King of the Cowboys. He earned his title because of his popularity with his public. Of course, Trigger's participation didn't hurt any either. Roy Rogers got his start when Gene Autry failed to show up for a scheduled picture shoot over a labor dispute. The studio cast Roy instead and the rest as they say.... is history. Roy Rogers got his start with Gene Autry in 1937 in *The Old Corral*. Roy had formed the band *The Sons Of The Pioneers* with actor Bob Nolan.

Roy was to make an appearance at the Greensboro Coliseum with The Greatest Show on Earth. My kids all owned horses and were huge fans of anyone on the silver screen who rode, especially Roy. I still had some connections with the office personnel at the Coliseum from my broadcasting days, so I got the ticket agent to wrangle some tickets to the show for the whole family. Everyone was so excited. We were going to see Roy, Dale and, most importantly, Trigger. This was a magnificent animal trained by Roy. He was not registered stock, his mother was a grade horse, she had no papers. Trigger's father was a registered thoroughbred. Roy taught Trigger 150 verbal and physical cues. In fact, Trigger had become such a showman when the crowd applauded, he would automatically take a bow. Actually, Trigger was a star long before Roy Rogers. He leased Trigger to the studios to be used in *The Adventures of Robin Hood* with Errol Flynn. Trigger was Olivia de Havilland's mount.

We were so excited when we arrived at the circus. We were going to see Trigger and Dale's horse, Buttermilk. Disappointment set in soon enough as it was discovered Trigger was not on the agenda. One of the producers had decided it would be a bigger hit if Roy rode one of the renowned Lipizzan Stallions that were in the show. The Lippizzans were one of the main attractions. I must admit even with the disappointment of finding out Trigger would not be in the show, I still felt giddy when they announced Roy would be riding one of those beautiful animals.

The Lippizzan Stallions are native to Austria. Most are white, but they have also spawned other colors. In the earlier part of this century the breed was owned and trained by the aristocrats of Austria. They were closely guarded, selfish in their ownership and adhered to strict breeding guidelines. It was rumored that General George Patton owned one of these animals when he was stationed in Germany. The breed became endangerd several times by war sweeping through Europe. The rescue of the Lippizzan Stallions during WWII by American troops was made famous by the movie *Miracle of the White Stallions*.

After WWII, the breed became available to the common man, if you could afford it. The average cost ranged from $2000.00 to $15000.00 based on blood lineage. They perform in four to six numbers and in close order drill, just like a drill team, in total unison. They are trained in both rein connection and leg pressure to perform their dance, so the rider must be well versed in both these functions in order to properly excute their talent.

It was quite a show. The King of the Cowboys and the world famous Lippizzan all on one ticket. My goodness, I was a kid again. We waited apprehensively to see Roy riding one of these legends as we enjoyed their unbelievable feats in the center ring. A normal horse will not get within fifty feet of fire, yet these horses were jumping through flaming hoops, rearing up, placing their hooves four deep on each other's back. It was an amazing performance. Instantaneous obedience to commands the human eye could not detect. The show must have lasted twenty to thirty minutes. The family anxiously awaiting Roy to come out on a white steed. We were sitting on the edge of our seats. Finally, the awaited moment was here. A drum roll, the crowd erupted and the King of the Cowboys wearing white hat, spangled suit, six shooters and fancy boots, rode into the center ring on a Lippizzan. We watched, amazed, and caught up in the moment. And then it happened. Putting the horse through his paces Roy must have touched the horse at the wrong pressure point because the horse went one way as Roy was headed in the other. Had he not been the great rider that he was, the headlines would have read "King of the Cowboys Bites the Sawdust". But he managed to decrease the space between the saddle and his posterior. I have no idea how he managed to do it, but the King of the Cowboys had pulled it off in first class fashion.

When Roy's estate was sold, at a New York auction, his favorite and most photographed saddle brought $50,000 and Trigger, stuffed brought in $266,000. Roy and Dale's 1964 bonneville sold for $254,000 (estimated to bring $ 150,000). Triggers saddle and bridle brought $386,000, one of Roy's many shirts brought $16,250. One set of boot spurs sold for $10,625, although no spurs were ever used on Trigger. Various chandeliers from the museum sold from $6875 to $20,000 as they were unique in their western style. A baseball autographed and given to Roy by Don Larsen after a perfect game against the Dodgers on October 8, 1953 sold for $2,500. A set of dinnerware along with the bible they used at the dinner table every night sold for $20,625. A fabulous painting of Roy, Dale, Buttermilk, Trigger and Bullet went for $10,625. An autographed picture to Roy from Gene Autry sold for $17,500. A Republic Productions Picture poster bearing many autographs of the people who starred in Roy's movies sold for $11,875. Dale's horse, Buttermilk sold below the pre-sale estimate for $25,000. Bullet, their German Shepherd sold for $35,000. Dale's parade saddle was estimated to bring $20000-$30000, sold for $104,000. Roy's script book for the January 14, 1953 episode of *This Is Your Life* sold for $10,000. A collection of memorabilia from his shows entertaining the troops in Vietnam sold for $938 with his flight jacket bringing $7,500.

Trigger was bred on a farm co-owned by Bing Crosby. Roy Rogers bought Trigger on a time payment plan for $2500 and then proceeded to make 188 movies together. Trigger won an Oscar for the movie *Son Of Paleface* with Bob Hope in 1953.

A COWBOY'S PRAYER

Roy Rogers rode the screen from 1942 until 1954 and for that twelve-year period remained Hollywoods biggest cowboy star. He had a deep religious faith, loved children and often walked Trigger up three flights of stairs to entertain the sick and terminal patients. Trigger's real name was Golden Cloud, but on the suggestion of one of Roy's co-stars, changed it to Trigger, because he was so fast not only in speed, but also in learning abiliity. Trigger lived to be thirty-three years, old succumbing in 1965. Roy passed away July 6, 1998 and his wife, Frances Gofavia Smith, known to most as Dale Evans died three years later on February 7, 2001. Below is my personal photo of Roy and Trigger;

Roy Rogers and Trigger

When people think of you, they will never remember you as Leonard Slye from Ohio, for you will forever be known as Roy Rogers, King of the Cowboys and one of the most favorite memories of my lifetime.

JUDY – CAREER WOMAN

We had been in the chicken business for seven years. Judy was a very intelligent woman and she wanted to do more with her life than just raise chickens. She loved the farm life and she loved being able to care for the kids at home. But the kids were growing up; Marcy was almost a teenager.

Having a career of my own, I was very sympathetic to her feelings when she started looking for a job outside of the home. We had good friends, Laney and Rabbit, that lived close by and agreed to keep the kids after school for a few hours. Laney and Rabbit were an older couple that had never had children of their own. They welcomed our crew and treated them like they would have their own. The kids loved them just as much.

Judy had no trouble finding a job and went to work at Bio-Med Labs for Bill Irwin. Bio-Med was started by an Elon College professor Dr. James Powell. It started out dissecting frogs and has grown into the largest medical lab in the world. Unfortunately for Judy, Bio-Med had a reputation for its ridiculously low wages for hourly employees.

Bill Irwin succumbed to blindness at 28. He became world famous as the first and only blind man to ever walk the Appalachian Trail in a single season. It is a 2168 mile trek from Mount Katahdin in Maine to Springer Mouintain in Georgia. Bill took this journey with his Seeing Eye Dog, Orient. By the time he reached the Harpers Ferry in Virginia, the halfway point of his journey, he had become world famous. Bill wrote *Blind Courage* about his experience on the Appalachian Trail. A movie is currently in the works. Bill was a recovering alcoholic and a good christian man who influenced a great many people before he died of prostrate cancer on March 1, 2014.

Bonae Euliss Scholl, my niece by acceptance (Peggie's daughter), is constantly urging me to new challenges. I love her dearly. Bonae used to be an Allstate Insurance Agent. That was when the offices of Allstate were in the Sears buldings in a kiosk, although I don't think the word kiosk existed at that time.

As fate, or God would have it, Bonae was marrying an Allstate Executive and moving to Charlotte. She was tasked with the job of finding her own replacement. Knowing what a hard worker Judy was, Bonae contacted her and asked if she might be interested in the job. Well, saying Judy disliked change would be an understatement. I bet that woman agonized over that offer for three weeks. It was a commission job and Judy was afraid of the gamble. I kept telling her that as little as she was making at Bio-Med, this wasn't even a gamble. My words to her were simple "I know you, and you will make more money than you are making where you are now". She finally took the plunge.

Allstate sent her to school in Atlanta for four weeks. She seemed to be enjoying it but, in our conversations, she said it was rough. So much to learn and much like being in college. Classes all day, then hitting the books at night. As in everything else she attempted, Judy excelled and became the first woman in the Atlanta region to be awarded the Triangle Award. Allstate only gives the award to the top person in the class.

THE SALESMAN

I had to decide what to do with my life. I had spent the better part of my time in broadcasting. I guess every news anchor is a salesman in their own way, so sales would be the natural progression. I went to work for Oakwood Homes, starting in the Burlington location. I transferred to Raleigh shortly after beginning with them, where my title on most sales in a month still stands undefeated. I worked for Bob Browning. If ever there was a man that had his head screwed on straight, it was Bob. I don't remember him ever being down about anything in life, the entire two years I worked for him. Bob was a salesman's salesman and always very comfortable at the trade, very likeable and personable and took the Raleigh sales center from the bottom to the top five. By doing so, he had become a legend in the company. Bob was always dangling the carrot in front of you without you being fully aware of what he was doing. That never bothered me because if there was something I wanted and Bob found out about it he would say, "C'mon Gene, let's go for ride". The next thing I knew we were in a store looking at whatever I had told him I wanted. He'd say, "You sell six homes this month and I'll buy it for you". I think the only goal he ever set for me that I did not meet was an upright tool box which back then was around $800, but I came close.

I lived about an hour from the sales center and made use of the drive by listening to motivational tapes to get my day started off right. Most of th time, when I got to work, I would bounce in the front door singing James Brown's, "I Feel Good". Bob loved it because he knew enthusiasm was contagious. I was having one of my rare bad days and Bob having this innate ability to sense when things were not on even keel with me said, "C'mon Gene, let's go for a ride". It was just after lunch on a beautiful sunny day and the next thing I know I'm flying over Raleigh looking down at the sales center. Bob owned his own plane and was an excellent pilot.

We flew around for an hour just enjoying the ride and leaving the reality of the real world behind. It was so exhilarating, I went back to the sales center and sold a couple of mobile homes that day. But such was the joy of working for this man. He always made me feel more like a friend than an employee and that made me want to help him succeed in any way possible.

After working for Bob for a year, he tried to convince me to move to Raleigh so I wouldn't have to make that trip every day. In true Bob Browing fashion, took me to look at a couple of farms, but I wasn't ready to leave Snow Camp. Bob is married to Debra, a beautiful girl. They have a son, daughter and one grandchild. Bob and Debra are two of my favorite people in the whole world, although I don't get to see them very much. They impacted my life at a time when I was having financial difficulties and through their motivation, helped me right the ship.

For the first five years at Oakwood, I stayed in the top twenty salespeople in the company. They offered wonderful incentives for high sales, including trips to various places and I always qualified.

AND WE TRAVELED

Judy and I traveled extensively at Oakwoods expense. We went to Hawaii, Jamaica, Hilton Head Island, Las Vegas and numeroius other places. It was like a Oakwood family affair; all the company executives went along. At Hilton Head, there was a huge party on the beach. The island is a gated community just outside of Charleston, South Carolina. We sat at a table with Nick Saint George, our CEO, my manager Boyce Roberts and his wife Margaret. We shucked and ate steamed oysters dipped in hot butter. For a while during the meal, I had it made as Nick would shuck one oyster for him and one oyster for me. I ate about a half a dozen before he turned the knife over to me to shuck my own.

The Hawaii trip was great as well. We had reservations at the Royal Hawaiian, one of Hawaii's landmark hotels. We took lessons on how to hula and I even brought back a grass skirt. I never understood exactly why they kept telling me "Watch the hands, that's where the story is". My eyes kept gravitating toward the hips. Guess that's why I never got the hang of it, but the native girls were experts. During the trip, Oakwood chartered a Catamaran and we sailed around Diamondhead where we saw beautiful homes, one of them was owned by Tom Sellock. He was living there while filming the television series *Magnum PI*.

The water of the pacific is so clear, you can wade up to your waist, drop a quarter, and see it fall at your toes. In downtown Honolulu, there is a strip mall named the International Market Place. There was no duty on goods brought back so Judy proceeded to shop 'til she dropped. Then we saw one of Hawaii's most famous entertainers, Don Ho. People came from all over to see him. When you went to see Don Ho, you never knew who may pop in. There were pictures of Don Ho with Dean Martin, Frank Sinatra, and the rest of the Rat Pack. It was a trip to remember for a lifetime.

In Las Vegas, we went to a live performance of Wayne Newton at Caesars Palace. Wayne Newton is a native of Sin City and after becoming extremely wealthy performing at Caesars Palace, purchased his own hotel and casino, the Aladdin. His performance was electrifying, and he never disappointed his fans. The curtain would open to fog, and a huge set of stairs. When the spotlight hit him, and he would come barreling down the stairs, belting out "Jack the Knife ", one of his biggest hits. Everyone dressed in suits and evening gowns and for one solid hour, we were spellbound, only moving to give mulitiple standing ovations during the performance.

Judy and I stayed at the MGM Grand Hotel, the hotel of the stars. Every room in the hotel was named after a star and ours was the Ava Gardner room. It was very appropriate since Ava Gardner was also from North Carolina.The MGM Grand was only a short walking distance from Caesars Palace, so it was easy to get to the Wayne Newton performance and back. Las Vegas is so lit up that even at midnight, it's like walking around in daylight. After the performance, on our way back to our hotel, I noticed news racks with free publications. Thinking it was a television schedule; I grabbed one and stuck it in my pocket and told Judy we could see what Vegas television had to offer. We got in our comfy clothes and I picked up the guide I had pocketed earlier and opened it up. Well folks, it made me blush. I was looking at a well photographed magazine, offering not a selection of ABC and CBS channels, but prostitutes. It came complete with telephone numbers and ways to pay via credit card machines. We got a big laugh out of it once we remembered that prostitution is legal in Nevada, and it pays to advertise. I guess that's the way to keep them off the street corners.

The next day we were feeding a couple of the thousand slot machines in our lobby. Judy was on my left playing a nickel machine and I, being the high roller of the family, was playing a quarter machine. There was an elderly lady on my right, playing three machines at once. These three machines just kept spitting out coins, so I asked her if she was winning. She replied, "Well Sonny, it depends on what time the plane leaves". Well, alright then.

Just then a siren and a bell went off. My first thought was somebody's robbing the place. Armed guards came running past us, from every direction. As you can tell from the next sentence not being, "We retired and never looked back", It wasn't us. But someone had hit the $35,000.00 jackpot.

Collection of Traveling pictures

We were in the lobby waiting on the bus to take us to the airport. I asked Judy to watch the bags for a minute, while I made one last attempt at the slot machines. I sat down at a fifty-cent machine. I had taken a thousand dollars with me for gambling and still had most of it with me. They were loading the bus when I inserted $0.50. That spin of the machine won me fifty dollars. I guess I can say I came home a winner. All that gambling and only fifty dollars better off. Guess the lady was right, it all depends on what time the plane leaves.

In Jamaica, there were vendors selling everything you could think of everywhere you went. I think marijuana and wooden sculptures was their mainstay. As we drove in to the hotel, I noticed there were telephone poles on both sides of the roads, but they had no wires on them. According to our cab driver, the poles were there to keep drug trafficers from landing on the highway at night.

The temperature in Jamaica is a constant seventy, breezy degrees. Our hotel was beautiful. There are no doors on the hotels, all the entrances are wide open. From our balcony you could see the ocean a short distance away with a beautiful array of palm trees and bougainvillea, a native plant of Jamaica. Huge rhododendrons were planted throughout the common areas in the hotel.

In order to capitalize on tourism, some of the natives built serenade rafts. The rafts had a seat big enough for two people. The captain stands behind the seat and guides the raft with a pole. It was a gentle, serene, peaceful, ride down the winding river. It was a beautiful and scenic view of the island countryside. Our guide gave us the history of the island as we traversed it. The Jamaicans are charming people and very resourceful. As a keepsake after our trip, we purchased one of the minature rafts from him. I look at it now and remember the wonderful trip.

While there, Judy and I, along with several other couples decided to go horseback riding along the beach. I know it's a surprising activity for us. We all rented horses which also came with a guide. We rode along the beach taking in the beautiful scenery. It reminded me of Ramey. All of a sudden, from out of nowhere, came this kid in his teens. He was dressed in a t-shirt, jeans and a baseball cap. We were surprised because it seemed he just materialized out of nowhere, but we weren't too concerned, as there were six of us plus our guide. He walked up giving us this big grin and in Jamaican lingo said "Ya mon, Wanna buy some smack?" As he was talking, he was waving a plastic bag full of marijuana for us to view. We all snickered, politely declined, thanked him for the offer and rode on. Only in Jamaica, Mon.

While there, we gathered the entire group of twenty and made the trip to the Cascading Waterfall of Ocho Rios, which travels for miles before emptying into the ocean. The falls were extremely slick, but we were resourceful people and formed a human chain, each person holding on to the next. It was so exciting, just a little risky. The day was a success as no one got hurt. Ochos Rios is famous for its appearance in the James Bond movie, *Dr. No*. Jamaica is also the first dry land Columbus set foot on in the new world.

Just before we left, I bought a hand carved bull. The dye on the bull was still damp, so I wrapped it in one of my t-shirts to keep from getting dye on my clothes. In Miami, we went through customs. The only thing they checked was my bull. The bull is about the size of a lap dog and being made from mahogany wood, has some weight to it. The customs agent said people would bore holes in the wooden sculptures, fill them with cocaine, and plug the hole. "Not me, Mon".

We had an hour layover in Atlanta. Anyone that's been through the Atlanta airport knows, even with the trams, you still walk miles to get from one plane to another. And here I was, carrying my treasured bull that's growing heavier by the minute. By the time I got home, I had the worst case of tendonitis in my forearm. I had to keep my arm in a sling for a week. But my treasured bull is still with me, sitting on my fireplace hearth.

JENNY

I sold a mobile home to a woman named Jenny. She was recently divorced with a small child, Frankie. She was a very personable woman who never seemed to meet a stranger. Something told me she could be a good salesperson. She was working with a financial firm at the time, struggling to make ends meet.

A year later, I was promoted to manager. My first responsibility was to find a replacement for my sales job. I contacted Jenny to see if she would have any interest in selling mobile homes. The first call I got a cool reception. But a good salesman never takes no for an answer. A few days later I called again and asked if she would mind coming to my office to discuss the matter. Something had transpired at her job that she wasn't pleased about, so she consented to the interview. I had my guns loaded.

After I told her all about the company, discussed the opportunities for monetary gains, and showed the possibilites for winning incentive trips, she was still a little hesitant. Being a single mother, the thought of going from a guaranteed salary to a draw plus commission was scary. I didn't push the issue and told her to think about it. She talked to her family and friends and everyone discouraged her from taking the job, but I had persuaded her, and she finally said yes. To me that meant important outside influences would not sway her, and she would not be so easy to give up on a sale.

Jenny worked for me for only a few years before she became my top salesperson. She was in the top twenty in the company consistently. She worked the hard, long hours the job required. Closings on homes would often come in the evening after customers got off work. That meant the salesperson would have to come back to the office in their off-duty time to close the deal. When a babysitter was not available, Jenny would come back with Frankie in toe to handle her responsibilities. A closing would take an hour or two, so Jenny would put little Frankie in a vacant office with his toys. Occasionally, he would get restless and sneak in my office. If it wasn't a busy evening, I would take him for a ride in my Corvette, because we all know little boys enjoy fast cars.

One day, Jenny took Frankie shopping with her. As most kids, Frankie always tried to come away from a shopping trip with a new toy. Jenny didn't deny him much, but this particular item was a bit pricey and it was so close to Christmas, she told him "No, I don't have any money right now". A move used by many parents when the word "no" does not suffice. She continued to explain to Frankie that when he grew up and had to make his own money, he would understand. Frankie, a sharp-and quick-witted child replied "Well I know one thing for sure; I'm not going to be a mobile home salesman. You never have any money!" Out of the mouths of babes. (I think Jenny made $13000 that month.)

There was a mobile home show in Raleigh. I went with one other salesman. An acquaintance of Jenny's came through looking at the homes. She asked if I had talked to Jenny. "No, I assume she's at the sales center, she had to open today." I was told she and Frankie had been involved in a head on collision with another vehicle. The other car had crossed the median onto Jenny's lane, hitting Jenny's truck. One of the three people in the other car had died. The impact had severed Jenny's foot almost completely from the ankle. Thank goodness for today's medicine. Pins and a cast combined with a great deal of courage, hard work and support and she was able to walk again. Oakwood continued to provide compensation for several years until she could return to work. Due to her ankle, she was never able to return to her sales job. It was the loss of a great career and a great employee. Jenny went back to school, graduating cum laude from Averett University in 2011 with an accounting degree. She now works in that field at a power company.

Frankie kept his word to his mom. He never became a mobile home salesman. All that playing in the dirt led him into a career in the heavy equipment industry.

MY LITTLE RUNAWAY

Judy worked several years while the chicken house sat empty until we finally decided it was time to sell the farm. We were approached by a couple that also lived in Snow Camp and just as Judy and I had been years ago, this couple was young and wanted in the farming business. We had lived on the farm for fourteen years. We raised cattle, dogs, horses, and kids, along with gardens, fields of oats and corn. We loved every minute of watching our children grow up on acres of land, free to roam the countryside on horseback and foot. You know the old saying "You can take the boy out of the country, but you can't take the country out of the boy."

After selling the farm, we moved to Gibson Road in Mebane, North Carolina. The property had a Tri-Level home and an inground pool along with a barn. The day we sold the horses was a sad day in all our lives, especially the kids. We hoped that having a pool, would in some degree, compensate.

Julie worshiped her mother and normally she and Judy got along exceptionally well. However, if you've had teenage girls, you know they are a little temperamental. Julie must have been around fifteen. I don't remember what started the argument between Judy and Julie, but it must have been a doozy. Julie stormed out of the house in a rage and marched down to the end of our driveway. Then she commenced to walk up the road. Judy watched her walk away and, in her mind, saw the 7 year old girl making her 100 yard dash, but this time, Cookie was not by her side. She worried for her daughter's safety and jumped in the car. She quickly caught up with her, rolled down the window and demanded that Julie get in. But Julie was having none of it and just kept walking, totally ignoring her mama. It must have been around 6 p.m. because just as Julie reached the peak of the curve in the road, she saw me coming home from work. Why is it that kids fear their father returning from work when they know they have done wrong? She wasted no time jumping in her mama's car. She knew she did not want to tangle with me. I think that was her final running away adventure.

WHO SHOT JR?

The Burlington Boys Choir was founded in 1959. It is a performing choir and a training group for boys in the Burlington area. The choir has traveled all over the world giving performances. In 1997, during the Clinton Administration, the Boys Choir sang at the White House. They also traveled to Europe on a ten day trip touring several countries, including Austria.

Miss Eva Wiseman directed the Boys Choir for 59 years. A long, long time ago, she even taught me; although I dare say not much of it took. I remember she was a stern taskmaster and demanded perfection from her students. She remained with the choir until her death in 2005 and is sorely missed by the City of Burlington.

Michael with Boys Choir

It was a distinct honor to be selected to sing in the Burlington Boys Choir. We were overjoyed when Michael was selected during his preteen year and it was an interesting experience. The Boys Choir had a demanding schedule that kept Judy and I about as busy as it kept Michael. If we had still been living on the farm, I don't think we could have ever made it happen.

They were a great bunch of kids that sounded like angels from heaven. Miss Wiseman had that group fine-tuned. Michael enjoyed the travel and the fellowship of the group. He stayed with the Boys Choir until he aged out.

Whenever there was a local concert, the parents came prepared. When a concert concluded, the parents would lay out a spread of food and snacks. As typical boys, they were always hungry. These were the 80's, the days of *Dallas* and JR Ewing. A group of us gathered one evening after a concert and stood around snacking on hors d'oeuvres when the discussion turned to Dallas, a common topic as it was the top rated show during that time. The previous week, the show had left with a cliffhanger. Someone had shot JR. JR Ewing was the guy everyone loved to hate. Well someone in the group was just crazy about the show and as the hour got later in the evening, commented "I wish we could move this along. I need to get home and find out who shot JR. I can't miss it". Not that who shot JR won't be a headliner in tomorrow's newspaper.

I guess if *Star Trek* fans can be Trekkies, JR Ewing fans can be Wingers. Judy and I discussed it the entire drive home and finally, shaking our heads in amusement, decided, to each, his own. Personally, I was always a Bobby fan, JR was just too sleazy a character for me. As Bubble Gum George used to say "he left his decency in the barn."

HEE HAW

Oakwood Homes used a company to set up the mobile homes, Ingle Movers, owned by Lonnie and his son, Eddie. We worked together for many years and became friends.

No one could accuse Lonnie of not enjoying life. Lonnie owned mules, so much so that when he passed away, the family placed oil paintings of his two mules on either side of his casket.

Lonnie's hero was Festus from *Gunsmoke*. Lonnie knew I loved to ride horses and often asked me to come riding with him and Eddie. This was one of the few times in my life that I didn't own a horse and had been without one for a year. No problem, Lonnie promised to supply the mount. When I got to Lonnie's, he and Eddie went to the barn and brought the saddled mounts back to the house. They were both snickering as I looked over my mount. I was supplied with a lovely Jackass, otherwise known as a Jenny or a Burro. This mule was so short, if I had been eight inches taller, the burro could have walked between my legs. Once Lonnie and Eddie regained their composure and finished laughing, we rode off into the woods down a long winding trail. Along the ride, we were having to lean sideways in the saddle because of the thickness of the trees. We came across a good size pine tree a storm had taken down right across our path. It was large enough we had to detour around it. Now, any experienced rider knows when a horse inhales, you tighten the girth. And I had assumed Lonnie had done the same with this beautiful stallion I was riding. The cinch held when I got on, but then again, that wasn't much of a stretch. Now folks, I may have jumped off a few horses in my life, but I've never fallen off a horse. We went around this downed tree; the saddle went under my jackass's belly and, BAM! I hit the ground. I forget the number one rule of riding—always check your cinch. At least I didn't have far to fall. I got up, tightened the cinch and continued on my journey. Being the comedian,

Lonnie asked if he needed to call the story into the news department. I just kindly thanked him for his generosity but told him I had just as soon this story not be on the news.

Lonnie, son and Gene on Mule

FREEMASONS

My grandfather and uncle were both Freemasons and I always aspired to be one. It is the largest fraternial organiization in the world and while it is not a secret society, it is a society with secrets. Dating back to the days of King Arthur and the Round Table, when the Christians and Moors were at war, its origin goes back even further to the days of King Solomon. George Washington, the father of our country, was the first freemason in the New World. Other famous names include John Wayne, Ernest Borgnine, Buck Taylor, Harry Truman, Franklin Roosevelt and Benjamin Franklin. It is an organization that is deeply rooted in the bible and bases its belief on the brotherhood of man and the sanctitiy of the family. Its charitable efforts circle the globe and affect many areas of mankind. The comrade of the freemasons is something extraordinary where the word brother really means something. You care for your brother and his well being; and the well being of his family. Each state is regulated by its own Grand Lodge and each state has its own history lessons. Our particluar grand lodge of North Carolina has chairs dating back to colonial times as well as numerous other artifacts.

I did not realize until later in life that I was never going to be invited to join, that "it is of your own free will and accord" that you petitiion this organization. The work schedule I maintained for most of my life kept me from joining the organization until much later in life. After attending for several years, I was voted in as secretary of the lodge, where I remained for seven years. I was honored and proud to be able to sit in the position of Secretary during my son, Michael's year as Master Mason. While in office as secretary, like everything else in my life, I jumped in with both feet. During my time as secretary, I created a wall to hang Past Masters pictures, pictures dating back to 1942 while another wall, pictures of the lodge officers coincide with those years. Alongside several brothers, we refinished and reupholstered a set of 100-year-old officers chairs from a Virginia lodge and before I stepped down as Secretary, my brothers voted me Secretary of Distinction.

Being presented the Secretary of Distinction Award by Michael

Some of the funniest things in life occur when you least expect them. I had recently purchased a new pair of florsheim boots. I hate breaking in new shoes, so I figured I'd wear them a few hours at a time and chose the bi-monthly meeting of the lodge to be a perfect place to start the process. Brothers always gather early before each meeting and can be found in the dining room waiting on prayer and dinner to be served. Food is layed out buffet style and we move down the aisle filling up our plates as we go.

I am never far from the front when it is time to eat and this time, I was third or fourth in line. Brunswick Stew was on the menu along with salad, bread, cake and ice cream. The elderly brother behind me was following along chatting with me as we filled our bowls. In one hand he carried his Brunswick Stew, in a much too small bowl, with his salad in the other. In addition to being small, the bowls were a little on the flimsy side. Well, gravity took control and my brothers bowl of brunswick stew landed on the top of my brand-new boots. Before I even knew what was happening, he was down on his hands and knees, wiping the stew off of my shoes, apologizing with every swipe.

I wasn't the least bit upset. I exclaimed "Quick! Someone get a camera, I want a picture of my brother shining my shoes". Someone commented later "Well that's one way to break in a new pair of shoes". This elderly man, whom I hold in such high esteem, came up to me after the meal and said "Gene, if I've ruined your shoes, I will be more than happy to buy you a new pair" As they were not the worse for wear, I brushed the comment aside. But being the brother he is, I have no doubt he meant every word of it.

Isn't life a hoot? You just can never take it too seriously unless you want to walk around with a bottle of Pepto Bismol in your pocket all your life. I'm sure if my brother buys this book, he will find the whole incident as laughable as I did. The worst thing that came from it was that we held up the line for a few minutes.

The Old Master's Wages

I met a dear old man today, who wore a masonic pin,
It was old and faded like the man, it's edges worn quite thin.
I approached the park bench where he sat, to give the brother his due,
I said "I see you've traveled east,", he said, "I have, have you.
Sometimes the greatest lessons are those that are learned anew
And the old man in the park today has changed my point of view
To all masonic brothers, the only secret is to care,
May you live your life upon the level, may you part upon the square.

I wish I had written this. It very well sums up what being a mason is all about.

America is the most charitable nation on the face of the earth and is always giving to a good cause. However, when giving, make sure you know where your money is going. Here are some facts you should know.

Remember, they are not completely up to date and I'm sure the names and figures have changed.

The American Red Cross President and CEO, Marsha J. Evans salary is $651,000 dollars a year plus expenses.

The United Way President Brian Gallagher has a base salary of $375,000 along with numerous expense benefits.

UNICEF (United Nations International Childrens Emergency Fund) CEO Caryl M. Stern receives $100,000 a MONTH plus expenses and a Rolls Royce. Less than $0.05 of your donated dollar goes to the cause.

The Salvation Army's commissioner Todd Bassett receives only $13000 per year plus housing for managing a two billion dollar a year operation. 96% of your dollar goes to the cause.

The American Legion Commander, the VFW Commander, the Disabled Amercian Veterans Commander, the Military Order of Purple Heart Commander and the Vietnam Veterans Association National Commander all receive zero, nada, zip, salary with all donations going to families and youth.

And the Masonic Lodge with all its worldwide lodges contributes two and a half million dollars a day to charities such as the Shriner's Burn Center, The Home for Chilldren in Oxford, North Carolina, cancer relief organizations with no administrative costs whatsoever. It's all voluntary. So next time you get that warm fuzzy feeling and want to help someone, make sure you know where your hard earned money is going and that is really going to make it to the people that really need it.

DID SHE ROB THE BANK?

Judy was always aware that I wanted a .30 caliber lever action western style carbine for the better part of my life. So without my knowledge and prior to the internet, she had been quietly looking around. We lived in the quiet, peaceful, sleepy, small town of Mebane. It's the kind of town in which most people would like to raise a family, and we were no exception. Judy visited a pawn shop, the only one in town. I'm sure it was a sight, a successful, prominent Allstate Agent drives up in her Cadillac to visit a pawn shop. It was gutsy. Women just didn't visit pawn shops but that didn't phase Judy one bit. The woman was fearless. She had called the pawn shop earlier. They had one and she wasn't about to let it get away.

She rushed to the store, delighted in her find. The salesperson showed her the lever action .30 cal. Winchester. It had a scope and a sling on it. The clerk asked if she wanted him to wrap it. Judy replied no, she would just carry it. So, my immacutely attired, prim and proper country girl, slung this gun over her shoulder, picked up her briefcase, and marched down the busy street in her suit and heels to her car parked about a half block away. People probably wondered if she'd just robbed the local bank.

She drew quite a bit of attention from local residents, but the looks from passerbys didn't phase Judy one bit as she marched down the sidewalk headed to her car.

MY PASO FINOS

The Paso Fino breed is of Spanish descent. The name is Spanish for fine pass, referring to their gait. They were brought to Puerto Rico by the conquistadors in the early sixteenth century. The pasos are used for cow ponys, trail riding and about anything else the Vaqueros, Spanish cowboys, wanted to use them for. They have tremendous endurance and much like the American Mustang, can run all day. A twenty-mile ride is a cake walk for these animals.

While in Puerto Rico, I grew to admire the Paso Fino breed tremendously. It's the reason I brought Rayo back to the States. There were a limited number of Paso Finos in the US. The horse appears to stand in one spot as he pitter pats down the road. The rider enjoys having no bounce. Other gaits they have is the paso quarte' and the paso Honduras, each a little bit faster than the one before. A good paso can reach speeds up to thirty miles per hour and never break his stride making for a smooth ride. The test of their smoothness is to place a glass of water on the saddle horn and complete a turn around the ring. Their action is akin to running in place.

Poco Dinero

I came across a Peruvian Paso Fino owned by a man in Reidsville, North Carolina. The horse's name was Poco Dinero, little money. He was a sorrel with a blaze face and four white stocking feet. I wasn't sure if his name meant he brought so little or was worth so little, but I realized quickly I should have changed his registered name to Mucho Dinero, much money. He was one of the finest horses I ever owned and was worth a lot to me. The Peruvian Paso has much of the same gaits as his counterpart, the Paso Fino, with one distinction. In his pace, he lifts his front two feet and flips them in an outward motion. It looks strange but has no effect on the smooth as silk gait. The Peruvian Paso migrated to Peru from Spain.

One of the things I learned about horses from George was to feed my horses well. I hated to see their ribs or their hip bones protuding. Often it would be weeks between rides and with most horses a generous feed and no exercise left them a bit rambunctious.

It had been my experience, horses that were allowed to wait that long between rides, would have to be exercised in a round pen or on a lunge line for fifteen minutes or so before saddling just to get the edge off them. Poco was the exception to this rule.

No matter how long I went between rides or how much I fed him, he was always the perfect gentleman when I threw the saddle on him. There was no balk leaving the barn, no shying at cars on the road. Even

18 wheelers didn't spook him. If ever there was ever a horse with a perfect attitude, it was Poco Dinero.

At the home in Mebane, North Carolina, there was 400 acres of undeveloped land across the street from us. It was a dairy farm. There were old logging roads on the acreage that made for perfect trail riding. Poco and I would hit the trails about three times a week. On this day we took one of the roads not traveled. It was a three mile stretch through what had become heavy underbrush. We came across a locked steel-cabled gate. The woods were far too thick to go around the cable. We were about thirty yards to the paved road which would lead us home so I urged Poco to step over the cable, not realizing its height because of the grown-up weeds. That's as far as he would go. I realized once I dismounted the cable was underneath his hind legs right at his sheath. With a great deal of effort on his part, I finally coaxed him over the cable. I mounted and headed to the barn. When I got home, I checked him good and saw no ill effects from the ordeal. I gave him a good rub down and his normal ration of feed. Poco always had a hearty appetite, so I cut off the light and bid him good night with a "Bon-appetite' ". Being a spanish horse, those were the only French words he really understood.

The next morning, I went to the barn to feed and let him out in the pasture. His bucket was still full with last nights feed. He nickered at me as usual, saying "good morning." He seemed okay so I turned him out to pasture and went to work, leaving his stall door open so he could get to his feed. That evening, when I came home, he was standing in his stall but still had not eaten. I called the vet who explained that he had an intestinal blockage. By now it was 6 in the morning. He had attempted everything he knew and recommended taking the 60 mile trip to the NC Veterinary School in Raleigh.

Julie and I immediately loaded Poco in the horse trailer and headed to the state capital, where the school was located. We stopped often to check on him as a precautionary measure, but Poco seemed to be faring well. Three miles from the school, we felt a bang from the trailer. I pulled over on the shoulder and we both jumped out and sprinted to the back. We found Poco hanging by his leather halter lying prone in the trailer. It would only be a matter of minutes before he would choke to death. With the speed only panic can summon, I whipped out my deer knife and cut the rope. Relief came immediately. Poco still did not get up. I had phoned ahead so the hospital was expecting our arrival. We jumped back in the truck and sped to the clinic. The staff was waiting on the loading dock and were able to get Poco on his feet and into the clinic. Poco died a few hours later of a ruptured spleen. I felt it was my fault for taking him across that wire, but the vet disagreed. Either way it was a quiet ride home that day without my friend.

NO COMB-OVERS IN THE POOL

One of the selling points of the house in Mebane was the pool. It was not uncommon to have half the neighborhood over, hanging out and enjoying it with the family. My son, Michael was fifteen at the time. I was starting to do the comb-over thing that men with (hmmm) thinning hair do. Men that are hoping to hang on to the last vestige of vanity. We used the pool frequently and on a beautiful, sunny Saturday afternoon I did a swan dive off the diving board, crossed the length of the pool, coming up at the other end of the pool. Right where Michael was sitting.

When I emerged from the water, straightening and placing my hands on my hips, all my hair was hanging down my back, my bald head glistening in the sunlight. Michael got a real charge out of that "Dad, why don't you cut all that off, it's obvious to everybody that you have no hair!"

I reminded him that his day would come, it was in his genes. I thought a lot that night about what he said and the next day, I stopped in at the barbers and had him shave the top and trim the sides. As I watched my life's efforts falling to the floor, I wasn't nearly as traumatized as I thought it would be.

Now, for you men who are still hanging on to your hair, rest assured, that while it is a high profile, physcological adjustment, once you become acquainted with the new you and get over the vanity part, you realize "I kind of like it". Consider the attributes of your magnanamous decision. No more hair spray, which to keep a perfect comb-over in place, can be expensive. No more combs, brushes or shampoo. There are less trips to the barber, and no need for a hair dryer. It's dry by the time you step out of the shower.

So, if you are thinning and baldness is inevitable, don't make the bogus hair restorers rich, just let it go. I found it to be a really smart choice. Wouldn't you rather look like Sean Connery than one of the Grateful Dead? Liberation, guys, liberation.

THE QVC QUEEN

Judy ran a successful Allstate Agency. Her name was proudly displayed on the prominent corner of Main and Pine Street. I was so proud of everything she had accomplished. In everything Judy set out to do, she accomplished with determination. Her sales reached such numbers that she was awarded a trip to Disney World. Michael had just started middle school and was at that perfect age to enjoy the trip, so the three of us made our plans. Just before leaving, Judy was diagnosed with a brain tumor. She would need surgery. My wife, with the news weighing heavy on her shoulders decided this trip to Disney was exactly what we needed.

After surgery, Judy recovered, and life seemed to return to normal. She continued to work full-time. Our perfect world was back. This would be temporary, as ten years after Judy's first surgery, we learned that the tumor was back. The second surgery was not as easy, and she was left with permanent side effects. Her equilibrium was off. She stumbled and was prone to falls. It took immense concentration to remember the things she had previously taken for granted, such as telling her left from her right. It became obvious that she would not be able to continue working. She left the agency and retired to our tri-Level house in Mebane.

In 1986, a new Channel aired on television, QVC. QVC stands for Quality, Value, Convenience. The channel brought products from the malls into our homes. It was a way for the retired and shut-in to shop from the comfort of home. Judy had always maintained a busy schedule. On the farm, she was raising kids and chickens while keeping the house in order and meals on the table. It only became more hectic when she pursued a full-time job outside of the home while keeping up with the kids, their schedules and the house.

Now, she found herself retired and unable to do the things she wanted to do. And she loved to shop. So, my beautiful Judy would sit in front of our television and place orders with QVC everyday. She was quickly crowned "The Queen of QVC".

All the kids had moved out, with lives of their own. Michael had finished his tour in the Marines and lived in my Mom and George's house as we had lost them both by this time. Pulling into the driveway for a visit, the first thing he saw were boxes on the front porch. All from QVC.

The second surgery had robbed Judy of her short-term memory, and as Michael brought the boxes in, it was like Christmas morning for Judy. She had no idea what she had purchased, so opening the boxes were as much a surprise for her and it was for me and Michael. One box contained in-soles for shoes. Judy proudly presented them to Michael. "Here, Michael, these are for you. They are supposed to make your feet feel wonderful." Michael looked at me and then to his mother. "Thanks Mom." He paused for a second. "They actually do work great, you gave me the exact same pair a few weeks ago." You couldn't help but laugh. Judy was always looking out for us all. I quietly took the package from Michael and boxed it up. It was not uncommon for me to return 5 or more packages to QVC in a week.

Judy eventually became wheel-chair bound. She had taken care of the family for so many years, it was time for me to take the reins, so I retired to care for her. It was difficult for her to get around the house with the different levels. We had lived in Mebane for 12 years, and as soon a I made the last house payment, we knew it was time to find a single level home.

RING THE DINNER BELL

Judy knew I would never be happy away from a farm, so we searched until we found an 18-acre farm on Deep Creek Church Road in Burlington. Julie lived close by and that ended up being a godsend in the years to follow. We purchased the farm and I proceeded to remodel, adding the necessary handicap accessories to make Judy comfortable. We added a large deck out back with a handicap ramp. The deck afforded a great view of the pasture. Twelve acres of fenced in, lush grass, and not a horse to eat it. Sixty days after closing on the home, we moved in.

Mrs. Clayton lived a couple of houses down Deep Creek Church Road. During the remodel, I was traveling from Mebane to the Burlington farm daily and noticed the horses in her pasture. I had lost Poco, and being without a horse, hers just seemed to call to me to stop and admire them up close. During my visits with her horses, I learned that the horses had been her husbands and she had lost him shortly before Judy and I bought the farm. Several months after after settling in at the Burlington farm, Mrs. Clayton called and asked if I could come by, assumingly to help with something around the house.

The next Sunday, we sat at her table and shared a cup of coffee and pleasant conversation before she asked if I would be interested in the horses that belonged to her late husband. She didn't want to sell them to just anyone and she felt I would give them a good home. When I inquired about the price, she promptly replied "They are not for sale, they are yours for free if you will give them a good home. They have been together for so long, they just have to go together." Before his death, Mr. Clayton couldn't speak loudly enough to call them in for feed. He had taught them to answer to an old farm bell. "You can have the bell as well as all the tack and farm equipment that goes with the horses." I was flabbergasted! We were talking about thousands of dollars in horses and equipment and she just wanted to hand them to me. I couldn't say no, so I thanked her for her generosity and planned to pick up the horses later in the week.

As fate would have it, I came down with an inner ear infection at the same time I planned to pick up the horses. The Clayton's lived close enough that I had planned to walk to the Clayton's farm and one by one, lead the horses' home. With a halter and a lead rope, I started walking the liveliest of the two back to the farm. I didn't get far. A short way up the road, the horse started turning me around and around in the middle of the road. It would have been bad enough for a healthy person, but with my ear infection, I got so dizzy dancing around in the middle of Deep Creek Church Road, I fell and lost the lead rope. That horse took off heading back to the Clayton's barn to join his mate. He was so fast, he could have won the Kentucky Derby.

Shaking off my woozy head and dusting off my knees, I headed back to the Clayton farm, caught the horse and put him back in the pasture. I explained everything to Mrs. Clayton, who was quick to inform me "You started with the wrong horse". I decided the best course of action was to find someone to help and lead both horses back to my farm at the same time. The horses eventually made it to the farm and as long as they were together those horses were gentle as lambs.

I mounted the bell on the barn and sure enough, when it rang, those two horses would come running, ready to be fed.

Mrs. Clayton and her daughter eventually moved back to her home place in New Orleans, Louisiana. Mrs. Clayton and her annual Christmas present of peanut butter fudge were greatly missed. Good neighbors are hard to come by.

Judy and I lived together at the farm in Burlington for 5 years. On Thanksgiving Day in 2005, surrounded by her family, the love of my life passed away. We were married for 40 years and I have wonderful memories of our life together. And those memories will keep me going.

THE HORSE BELONGED TO WHO?

I bought a mare from a woman at a horse sale in Archdale, a small town just outside of High Point. The mare had never had a colt, but she showed me the papers and said she thought the mare was in foal. I hadn't ridden in a few years, and while I had the space, didn't currently own a horse. I felt the mare would make a nice pasture ornament. I bought her, paying a little extra to deliver the horse to the farm. As I looked through the paperwork, I discovered the previous owner's name, Harold Traywick. Curious as to whether the mare was indeed in foal, I called directory assistance for the Troutman, North Carolina area and retained a telephone number. I was able to reach him and when I inquired about the mare; he remembered her and even remembered the date and stud that covered her. I was so excited and asked if I could visit him as he was only 2 hours away. Harold was open to the meeting, so on Julie's day off, we made the trip. Being Judy's daughter, our 2 hour trip took much longer. Julie, much like her mother would have, had to stop at every ice cream and hot dog stand as well as pottery shop we passed.

Harold Traywick lived a short distance out of the town of Troutman. I pulled in the driveway as he walked out of the house. The more we talked, the more we realized who we were talking to. As mentioned earlier in the book, actors sometimes changed their on screen names and Harold's son Randy, had been no different. Randy Traywick, known to his country music fans as Randy Travis had grown up in the home we were standing in. Well, Julie and I were in no hurry to leave and the congenial gentlemen seemed to enjoy our company. True to the south, he offered us some iced tea and gave us the tour. He showed us all the CMA awards Randy had won over the years. After our second glass of tea, we remembered why we were there and Harold took us to the barn to see Cash, the stud that covered my mare. Harold whistled and as we waited for the stud, the barn door opened and in walked a beautiful Palamino stud that would rival Trigger. Harold was an exceptional horse trainer and had trained Cash to open and close the barn door. Julie and I both fell in love with Cash who not only knew that trick but could lie down, roll over, sit on his haunches like a dog, and stand on a box on all fours. We were awestruck. I couldn't get Harold to disclose any of his training secrets but, like George, believe he was a true horse whisperer. I asked him if he had any interest in selling Cash and he said Randy had left Cash to his grandson who was living with him.

Talk about one of lifes great adventures right in your own backyard. Julie and I took numerous pictures with the horse while Harold, like a proud father, put him through his paces. Julie talked non-stop about that horse all the way home.

Just before I bought the mare, I had completed the tack room in the barn. There was a wood stove, bar, television, hardwood floors and a sink with hot water. I had a bunk bed in case I had to stay out there for the duration. It even had a poker table I had purchased from a friend. I watched the mare carefully over the next few months. Harold had told me it was a good possibility the foal would be a palamino and when the foal should arrive, so I was counting the days. This was her first colt and it can sometimes be a frightening thing for a mare. I wanted to be close just in case. She had a paddock connected to the barn with free access to her stall. It was a chilly morning and I checked on her before coming to the house to get a few hours sleep. When I went back out, she had already breeched and the colt was coming. I phoned the vet and Julie who lived close by and was an experienced vet tech. They both arrived quickly and while the vet was able to save the mare, the colt was still born. Julie bawled for hours. I buried the colt on the the farm and continued to monitor the mare. She wouldn't come to the barn to eat and would lay out in the pasture at night instead of coming to the barn. I guess her grief over the loss of her colt was too much and it was like she blamed me. We never bonded and I sold her shortly after.

Bunk House, Harold and Cash, Cash

COWBOYS LOVE THEIR PEACH COBBLER

Salisbury, North Carolina holds a National Shooting Event. People come from as far away as Florida. It was a cold wintry Saturday when Darryl Allen, Lee Elliot, Tommy Allen and I climbed out of Lee's car. We were all cowboyed up in our western attire and Stetson boots. It had been a two-hour journey and we had reminisced about our school days the entire way. We were all wannabe cowboys and Lee had mentioned that occasionally a real cowboy may attend the Salisbury function. Tommy, in his youth was serious about learning the art of the quick draw and still carries a slug in his right knee from his training. I must admit, I practiced the art as well, but my gun was always unloaded. For some, that skill takes a lifetime to learn. That would be both the skill of the quick draw and the skill of unloading your gun before you practice a new skill.

During the ride, we talked of old movies and had a lot of sentences that began with "Do you remember?" I told them the names of the horses of the cowboy stars; The Duke's Appaloosa was named Cochise, Jimmy Stewart always rode the same horse, Pie. Sunset's was Cactus, Randolph Scott's was Gyp and followed him around like a puppy. Roy had Trigger, Dale had Buttermilk. Rocky Alan Lane had Blackjack. So many memories and so many laughs.

Pictures from the National Shooting Event

The shoot was in a huge open field with eight to ten cut-out areas with burms. Burms are 15-foot-high walls of dirt behind the target that's used to stop the ammo from going further. Some of the nations top shooters came from all over to participate in the event. It was obvious from their campers, rigs and hardware, they had a lot invested in this hobby. Women and men waited their turn to shoot. One woman, from Florida allowed me to look at her chrome-plated, pearl-handle, .45's. She was outfitted in western chaps, boots, spurs and a stetson. Annie Oakley would have been proud. She and her husband had made a bundle in the stock market, retired in their 40's and now were traveling around the country in their RV.

The guys and I split up, walking around checking the various vendors from everywhere. You could find everything from western wear to leather goods, holsters and guns. After a few hours, we met up. Our feet were killing us when we noticed the chuck wagon man had some chairs and a couple of stools around the camp fire. We asked to join him, and he offered to share his campfire. He had erected a tripod over the fire with a shallow cast iron pan. That pan was giving off a wonderful smell. We inquired as to its contents and surprisingly he said, "Peach Cobbler". He offered to give us a sample when it was done. He wasn't getting rid of us now.

There was a chilly wind blowing across the open field, but it was warm and cozy in the sunshine by the fire. We sat around and chewed the fat. The more the the chuckmaster talked, the more fascinating he became. He had been to Hollywood, where he and his wagon had taken bit parts in some westerns. He relayed to us the western stars he knew personally along with their pictures. We chewed the fat for another hour, before he got up, checked the fry pan and announced proudly that the cobbler was ready. He dished each one of us out a healthy portion and gave us a plastic fork. Normally, he sold the cobbler, but refused to take our money. I gotta tell you folks, that was the best peach cobbler I have ever tasted, and my mom was an expert. Maybe we were just hungry, maybe it was because it was cooked in an iron skillet over an open flame, or maybe he just had the touch. But as Andy Griffith would say it was "gooo-oood"

We left for home, a new adventure and a wonderful memory with old and new friends. The world is indeed, a fascinating place.

COWBOYS WITH COMPUTERS

Michael has always loved computers and technology. Judy and I bought him a Commodore 64 when he was a kid and he's been in love with the growing technology ever since. Unfortunately, the Commodore 64 is the extent of my training in computers. My son will quickly tell you that I know just enough about computers to be dangerous. Michael, along with a buddy opened his own business, ReliaSys Techologies in 2013. The company is growing and expanding every year. As a completely unbiased, proud father I have to say he is great at what he does. I don't know exactly what it is, but everytime I call him, he makes everything work right again.

Michael at his Commodore

I am baffled by computer terminology. Michael once told me my computer crashed. I said "son", I use that term of endearment when I have a computer issue, it makes it more family-like so he won't charge me. Son, I said "My computer doesn't crash. It may sashay, amble or mosey but it definitely doesn't crash." It's hard being a cowboy in a high tech world.

I often wonder how this generation is going to adapt to future generations and what will then be new technology to them. They will probably go kicking and screaming just like we are doing. I have a good friend who to this day refuses to text on his cell phone. Personally, i'm not kicking quite that hard yet.

I got to thinking about a senior's version of modern day technology and my thoughts are these:

Technology term	Senior Interpretation
Floppy Disc	Vertebrae keeps moving around
Hard Drive	Long trip with no pillows
Pdf	Abbreviation for pretty darn funny
Microsoft	Lets talk quietly about little things
Hard copy	Let me get my glasses
Facebook	Got my picture on the cover of time
Email	Everybodys writing to me
Google	Makes the baby laugh every time
Antimalware	What my Uncle prefers his wife not buy
Recycle bin	Then we can recycle Tom, Dick and Harry
Shortcut	Refrain from going the extra mile
Mail merge	USPS, Fedex, and UPS are joining forces
JPG format	Just plain good
TIF format	Technically its foreign

If I apply the principle of Facebook to my life, I would walk down the street and tell passerbys what I have eaten, how I feel, what I did the night before, what I will do later and with whom. I would give them pictures of my family, my dog, of me gardening, taking things apart in the garage, having lunch and doing what anybody and everybody does everyday. I would listen to their conversations with an "atta boy" and tell them I like them. This would be just like Facebook except I would probably have a couple police officers, a private investigator and a physchiatrist following me around.

LEARNING A NEW LANGUAGE

I'm assuming most of the folks who will read this book are either educated or seeking more knowledge of some furtherance. There are readers and there are readers. I can speak enough Spanish to get by and a sprinkling of French from high school, "Parlez vous francais?" And the answer, of course "No, Chevrolet Coup-e". Anyway, at this stage of life I have become concerned about the condition of my teeth, although I don't know why as they will probably outlive the rest of me. Be that as it may, I have recently enrolled in the School of Dentistry at UNC-Chapel Hill, probably one of the finest dental schools in the country. Now, I have to tell you, I was a little apprehensive about a kid using my mouth for a sandbox, but nonetheless, took the plunge. I've now found that they are the greatest people in the world, next to the VA. If only they will continue to treat their patients in their private practices the way they are trained, the future of dentistry is promising.

After several visits, I have come to realize that about anyone with a DeWalt drill can become a dentist. Camping inside someone's mouth for an hour or two is the easy part. The hard part is learning to speak dentistry. Denistry is a foreign language all its own and known only to the deep dentistry state. One of my teeth had to be capped and my student dentist is William. William is a terrific young man and will become a very successful dentist in another year or two.

At any given appointment, you may see as many as three to four dentists per visit, usually two students who do the work, a consulting dentist and the supervisor, otherwise known as the teacher. And they are all having fun stretching your mouth. Meanwhile, you are just lying there in total ignorance of the conversation going on around you. I felt like an angel looking down on the group. And it wouldn't have mattered anyway because I don't speak dentistry. The teacher was explaining to William what steps he should take and how much more drilling he needed to do. At this point, I chimed in "Please don't encourage him any further". Well, they just ignored me and continued to talk in dentistry. I have come away with the definite knowledge that dentistry is another language and to be a dentist it has to take years of learning the language. Drilling is the easy part.

Just before they were ready to cap my tooth and were giving my mouth a much needed break, the teacher was going through the process in a highly sophisticated terminological explanation of what final touches William needed to do prior to capping the tooth. They were looking at the computer monitor while I sat quietly waiting for them to dissect me. I had absolutely no idea the meaning of anything they had said but as soon as the teacher finished his lengthy explanation to William, I once again chimed in "Doc, that's exactly what I told him to do, but you know how kids are these days, he wouldn't listen to a word I said". I guess I didn't speak good dentistry, but I'm afraid that's one language I could never learn. But I'm gonna hang on to my DeWalt drill, just in case.

NEWS EVENTS THAT AFFECTED MY LIFE

Three major news events stand out in my life as the most memorable; the assassination of President John F. Kennedy, the landing on the moon and the 2001 terrorist attack on the World Trade Center.

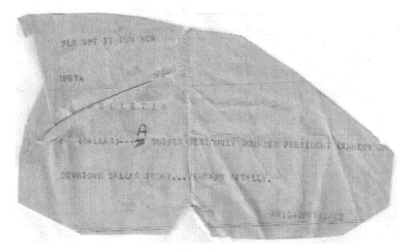

News of Kenndy's death

I had been working a short time at WBAG radio in the Spring of 1963. I was going to have lunch with Mom and was listening to our frequency when the news broke that Kennedy had been shot. I was so stunned, I had to pull over and collect my thoughts. I called the radio station to see if they needed me. When they said no, I proceeded to Jims Tastee Freeze to meet mom. I kept the orginial UPI bulletin copy announcing the shooting. It happened at 12:40 p.m. on November 22nd. I had that bulletin in my possession for some sixty years. I also have an audio tape of a minute by minute description of the event by CBS Cub News Correspondent Bob Schiefer, covering one of historys greatest happenings. I kept the tape but have since sent it to the congressional archives in Washinton D.C. They informed me that although they had several copies from other networks, this was the only one from CBS. I was glad to donate it for Americans and historians to enjoy.

We had just purchased our first black and white television when Walter Cronkite reported the nations landing on the moon. What a treat as Neil Armstrong proclaimed, "One small step for man, One giant leap for mankind". No one realized the enormous possibilities this event would open for the world.

And then we have September 11, 2001. Nineteen militant muslims hijacked four Boeing airliners and flew them into the World Trade Center and the Pentagon. Thanks to the bravery of its passengers, one crashed into an empty field in Pennsylvania or it may have been the White House.

It was about 8:45am. I was just heading over to see my son, Michael, at his office and have breakfast with him. I had been retired several years by then. I heard the news break on the radio. I assumed it was an accident. By the time I had reached Michael, the second airliner crashed into the tower. I knew, then it was no accident, that America was under attack.

The traumatic effect on the computer in our skull is amazing when events of such enormous magnitude occur. It brands a place in your memory for life that you can never erase. And now, eighteen years later, we are still fighting the remnants of that event.

So many stories came out of the events that occurred on September 11, 2001. Late Tuesday morning on September 11, Liuetant Heather "Lucky" Penney was sitting on the runway at Andrews Air Force Base with her hand on the throttle of an F-16 fighter. She had orders "Bring down United Airlines Flight 93". The days fourth hijacked plane seemed to be hurtling toward Washington. Penney says "she geniunely believed this would be the last time she ever took off". The one thing she didn't have was ammo or missiles. Her intent was to use her plane as a kamakaze. The surprise attacks were unfolding faster than they could arm the planes, so Penney and her commanding officer planned to fly their jets straight into the Boeing 757. As it unfolded, some hours later, Lieutenant Penney would eventually escort Air Force One back into Washington's severely restricted air space.

Penney was sitting around a briefing table at air combat training in Nevada when someone announced a plane had hit the tower. They assumed it was an accident until the second plane hit. They knew it was war. The surprise was complete, everything was confused, nothing was ready. Jets were still equipped with dummy bullets for training missions. This scenario has now changed and today there are two "hot-cocked" planes ready at all times, their pilots never more than a few yards away.

"Lucky, you're coming with me" barked Colonel Marc Sasseville as they were getting into their flight suits. As their eyes met, he said "I'm going for the cockpit." Without hesitating Penney replied, "I'll take the tail". It was a plan and a pact. Ignoring the normal flight list check for pilots, her crew chief pulling out the safety pins as she started rolling, she whispered a fighter pilots' prayer "God, don't let me (expletive) up "and followed Sasseville into the sky.

Penney and Sasseville knew their chances of ejecting and succeeding were extremely slim. They were more afraid of failing than dying. As it turned out, she didn't have to knock down an airliner full of kids, salesmen and girlfriends. It was hours before they learned of the insurrection by the passengers that brought the plane down. The passengers on that plane had been willing to do just what the two guard pilots were planning to do; anything and everything. Penney says the real heroes were the passengers, that she was just an accidental witness to history. She still loves to fly and still thinks often of that extraordinary ride down the runway a decade ago that could have been her last.

THE HOME STRETCH

I lived at the farm on Deep Creek Church Road for 14 years. The last few years were tiring, to say the least. The daily upkeep was too much for a young man to handle, much less a man in his senior years. The horses were gone and the fields were growing up. I came to the realization that it was time for a more manageable place. Fortunately, the perfect house became available within walking distance of Michael's and after a very short remodel; I sold the farm and moved back to Graham.

I realize that in my 80 years, my life has come full circle. I have returned to the area where my adult life began. I am not even a mile from the first home I purchased and rebuilt, the house I traded for the farm where Judy and I raised our kids. I'm steps from the home I lived in when I returned from service, the house now owned by my son, Michael, and his wife, Tracy.

Although I no longer have horses, I can sit on my back deck and have my morning coffee while watching my neighbors' horses in his pasture. I get to enjoy all of the beauty of the animals with none of the upkeep.

Well folks, it's been a hoot. I have thoroughly enjoyed writing this book, because the bulk of it I have lived. I sincerely hope you have enjoyed the reading as much as I have the writing. When you get down to what I call the home stretch, you begin to wonder about all the things in life you have done, or haven't done, people you have met or haven't met, and wonder if you would change anything given the option. I'm pretty sure everyone would make some of their decisions a little differently given the opportunity. For the most part, I have very few complaints. If possible, we all make of our lives, what we want them to be.

I have tried to live my life so that people who knew me would respect me, which to me is every bit as important to me as being well liked. I think I have earned the respect of my family and peers by my actions, which is also important. But I think as I said in the foreward of this book the most important thing to me was my own self respect. So many of today's young people have lost that. They don't respect themselves and who they are, so how can society expect them to respect others. This isn't a race issue, it's a universal problem. I think the Duke put it aptly in his last movie *The Shootist*, when he was asked by Ron Howard about his code of life. He said, "I won't be insulted, I won't be laid a hand on, I don't do these things to other people and I require the same from them". Respect, for yourself and for your fellow man, is desperately needed again in our world. And respect must be taught from the womb to the tomb. And if they don't fear man, they better fear God. The government, through their social programs has hamstrung families to the point they can't even discipline their own children without fear of reprisal. The children get the attitude they can get away with whatever and need not fear retribution. Meanwhile, parents, out of either a misguided sense of love and affection, or just a slovenly attitude seemed to have stopped caring. They no longer want to discipliine their children so they leave it up to society. I'm talking tough love here, not child abuse.

My children were taken in tow when they were growing up, usually when their mama's tactics didn't take care of the situation. It measured discipline and I know from the way they turned out that it works.

I look at our educational system. The more money we pour into it to make it better for our children, the worse it gets. I read news articles on the internet, and the news reporters can't even spell words correctly. I'm constantly finding words used incorrectly, sentences not grammaticly correct, or words that do not fit where they are placed. I remember when you would have to stand in the corner for five minutes if you misspelled a word. What in the world is the point in learning another language if you can't even get your own language right. I guess as the preacher says "I've quit preaching and gone to meddling".

I realize we will never again have things the way they once were. It's good and it's bad. We have given up a lot of the finer things in life in the name of progress. Technology has consumed the world to the point; we don't slow down long enough to have a conversation. We text, facebook, phone or don't communicate at all. I read somewhere the best classroom in the world is at the feet of grandpa/ grandma. Oh! They probably can't tell you about algorithms or pi=mc square. All their pies were round, but they can give you a lot of lifes common sense. I mean let's face it, if experience counts in life, then who has more experience than someone who has been around for seventy five or eighty years. They can tell you more of what not to do than anybody on the planet, because they've probably already made the mistakes themselves.

Often, radio broadcasters will end their shift with a sign off song. When I was stationed in Ramey, working in Armed Forces radio, I pulled the late shift from 9 til midnight. My sign off song was "Through the Years" by Kenny Rogers.

As the song ended each shift, my final words were always "Good night Judy, wherever you may be". I guess wherever I was; she was always in my heart. And wherever I go, she will remain; always in my heart.

My sincerest wish for each and every one of you is good health and much happiness; peace and prosperity; and the saving knowledge of our great creator. May he continue to bless this great country we call the United States of America.

CHAPTER 6

PROOF THAT LIFE'S A HOOT

BILLY GRAHAM

This is a terrific story about Billy Graham in the year 2000. Leaders in Charlotte, North Carolina invited their favorite son to a luncheon in his honor. Billy hesitated to accept because of his struggle with Parkinson Disease, but the Charlotte leaders said, "we don't expect you to speak just come and let us honor you". So he agreed. After numerous accolades were accorded him, Dr. Graham stepped to the podium, looked at the crowd and said "I'm reminded today of Albert Einstein, the great physicist, who this month was honored by Time Magazine as the man of the century.

Einstein was once traveling from Princeton on a train when the conductor came down the aisle punching the tickets of every passenger. Einstein looked feverishly trying to locate his ticket looking in all his pockets, but to no avail. Finally, the conductor said "Don't worry about it, Dr. Einstein, we all know who you are, i'm sure you bought a ticket. Don't worry about it. Einstein nodded appreciatively and the conductor continued down the aisle. As he was getting ready to enter the next car he looked back and saw the great physicist down on his hands and knees looking under the seat for the ticket. The conductor rushed back and said "Dr. Einstein, I know who you are and i'm sure you bought a ticket. Einstein replied "young man, I too know who I am, what I don't know is where i'm going.

Having said that Billy Graham continued. "See the suit i'm wearing. Its a brand-new suit. My wife, my children and my grandchildren are telling me I've gotten a little slovenly in my old age. I used to be a bit more fastidious. So I went out and bought a new suit for this luncheon and one more occasion.

You know what that occasion is? This is the suit in which I will be buried. But when you hear that i'm dead I don't want you to remember the suit that i'm wearing. I want you to remember this. I not only know who I am…. I also know where i'm going.

William Franklin Graham Jr. born on Nov. 7th, 1918. The North Carolina native from Montreat reached over 2.2 billion people worldwide during his ministry. He was spiritual adviser to every president going back to the 33rd President Harry Truman. Because of his worldwide crusades he preached the gospel in person to more people than anyone in the history of christianity. He once turned down a five-million-dollar contract from NBC to continue his touring revivals. One revival at Madison Square Garden ran nightly for sixteen weeks or 112 nights non-stop. The largest revival he ever held was on the great lawn of New Yorks Central Park in 1998 where a quarter million people attended. Dr. Graham died Feb. 21, 2018 at the age of 99.

IN 1913

Henry Ford set up his assembly line and was paying the highest wages in the country at 5.00 per hr.

The worlds largest power dam, the Keokuk Dam, opened, spanning the Mississippi River from Keokuk, Iowa to Hamilton, Illinois.

A loaf of bread cost $0.06, a gallon of milk $0.36, a pound of butter $0.38, a new Ford $490, a gallon of gas was $0.12, a new home $3395 and the annual income was $1236.

Jules Goux broke the speed record at the Indianapolis 500 with a win at an incredible speed of 76 mph.

Philadelphia beat New York in the World Series sweeping it in four games.

Democrat Woodrow Wilson was President with Thomas Marshal as his Vice President,

The top song was *You Made Me Love You* with Joe McCarthy and James Monaco

Favorite box office stars were Charlie Chaplin and Douglas Fairbanks Sr.

It will be 14 more years before the advent of the academy awards for best actor and best actress.

I guess in the grand scheme of things everything is relative. Now we make $25000-$50000 and pay $150,000 for a house and $45000 for a truck.

ACCIDENTAL GUN DEATHS

Some facts to ponder, according to Health and Human Services, there are about 700 thousand doctors in the US and accidental deaths caused by those doctors are around 120,000, or 0.171 deaths per physician. There are 80 million-gun owners and according to the FBI, there are 1500 accidental deaths by guns, in all age groups. So statistically speaking, doctors are 9000 times more dangerous than gun owners. So, guns don't kill people, doctors do.

Fact: Not everyone has a gun, but everyone has at least one doctor. Please alert your friends, we must ban doctors before this gets out of hand. I have withheld statistics on lawyers for fear everyone would panic and seek medical attention.

WHAT DID YOU SAY?

I think God gave us a sense of humor for a purpose and I think in times of stress, it becomes a pressure relief valve. There is still a lot of good, clean humor in the world and a lot directed at senior citizens, but what the heck "Life's a hoot" right. This ought to get your day going. One of my classmates, Larry Horner sent me these.

Three old guys are out walking. First one says "Windy, ain't it?" Second says "No, it's Thursday" and the Third one chimes in with "So am I, let's go get a beer".

A man was telling his neighbor "I just bought a new hearing aid and it cost me four thousand dollars, but it's state of the art...it's perfect". "Really?", answered the neighbor "What kind is it?" the man replied, "Twelve thirty".

Jason, an 82-year-old man, went to the doctor to get a physical. A few days later, the doctor saw Jason walking down the street with a gorgeous young woman attached to his arm. A couple days later, the doctor spoke to Jason and said "You are really doing great, aren't you? Jason replied, "Just doing what you said doc, get a hot mama and be cheerful". The doctor said "I didn't say that, I said, you've got a heart murmur; be careful ".

As you know, hospital regulations require a wheel chair for patients being discharged. While working as a student, a nurse found an elderly gentleman already dressed, sitting on a bed with a suitcase at his feet, who insisted he didn't need help leaving the hospital. After a chat about rules being rules, he reluctantly let the nurse wheel him to the lobby. When they got there the nurse asked if his wife was meeting him, to which the elderly man replied "I don't know, she's still upstairs in the bathroom, changing out of her hospital gown."

Two elderly gentlemen in a retirement home were sitting on a bench under a tree. One says to the other, Jim, I'm 85 years old now and just full of aches and pains. You're my age, how do you feel?" Jim says "I feel like a newborn baby, no hair, no teeth, and I think I just wet my pants".

An elderly man went to the doctor with hearing problems and got fitted for a new hearing aid, improving his hearing to 100%. He went back in a month and the doctor said his hearing was perfect and his family must really be pleased. The gentleman replied "Oh, I haven't told them yet, I just sit around and listen to conversations. I've changed my will three times.".

We may be old but we're not stupid, how do you think we made it this long?

RAMBLINGS OF AN OLD MAN

Practically every household in America has a least one dog, and most have multiple pets. Have uou ever stopped to think what dogs must think of us? I mean we come back from the grocery store with the most amazing haul of chicken, pork, and a half a cow. I bet their reaction is "Wow my owners are the greatest hunters in the world". Of course, let's not forget the feline population. Men have to understand something. Women and cats are going to do just as they please, so men and dogs should relax and get used to the idea. Dogs are wonderful companions, for a boy. They teach him fidelity and preserverance and to turn around three times before lying down. One of the main reasons a dog has so many friends is because he wags his tail and not his tongue.

When we lived in the country, I hunted for deer and like most deer hunters I would get up around 4am to head into the woods. A lot of times, the deer had to know I was coming. Now, it's a lot easier to bag one, just drive down the road in your car and they'll find you.

I realize I'm kinda rambling, but please bear with me. Some days your mind just works that way. Do you remember the Y2K threat, when everyone believed all the worlds computers would shut down when the date hit the year 2000? Banks were scrambling, people got rich selling preventative gadgets. Nothing happened. Maybe it should have been called UB1-2.

When Bobbie Martin was covering the High Point beat, she tells this story. The police had picked up several suspects and had them in a lineup. The Sergeant was going down the line asking them to repeat a phrase for the viewing witness. The phrase was "Give me all you money or I'll shoot". As they got to the fourth suspect, the sergeant reiterated the phrase. About that time, suspect #2 pops up and says, "That's not what I said". Truth is definitely stranger than fiction.

I guess this must be my humor day in writing this piece. What I am passing on to you now is not my original information, so I hope I'm not plagiarizing. It's probably doubtful since this stuff is about thirty years old, with no known author.

I am sure you have heard the term "the generation gap". Well technology has furthered that gap extensively. I got to thinking about this, the older you get the more philosophical you get, and realized just how much of a language barrier computers have made in our society. It must have been a really slow day, since I decided to explore this train of thought in further detail. Now, for all you senior citizens reading this, here's what I came up with:

1. A joint was a place where we used to hang out and have a drink.
2. A bong is what happened to your head when your Dad took you in hand.
3. Ecstasy was a passionate night with a hot little number.
4. A mouse was something you caught in a trap not played on your desk.
5. Channel surfing you did in the river because you couldn't afford the beach.
6. Download was an experience on the throne aka the toilet.
7. A virus was something like an ego that made everyone sick except the owner.
8. Don't you love it when it says windows will now check your disc, didn't know mine had slipped.
9. When recycle bin meant you gave Ben, the kid next door, your old bike.
10. When tailgating was following a pickup too closely.
11. Mad cow disease was getting in the wrong bulls pasture.
12. If it started tweating, we put WD40 on it.
13. High blood pressure was if you were breathing above the 119th floor.
14. A cell phone was your first call from jail after you were arrested.

Now that I'm older I have discovered the following. Hopefully, they will make you grin or take your mind off your problems for the day.

1. Most of what I started out with, I still have; which is nothing.
2. After sewing my wild oats, I now find they are prunes and all bran.
3. I got my head screwed on straight, but now my body is a wreck.
4. I can't seem to remember things like I used to.
5. I can't seem to remember things like I used to.
6. Well it's an official fact, life is definitely unfair.
7. Whoever's passing the buck, I hope it stops here.
8. I plan to get on the comeback trail as soon as I fugure out where I've been.
9. Everytime I get a great poker hand, everybody wants to play another game.
10. A grave is a rut with both ends closed off.
11. The hereafter comes to mind a lot. Like I wonder when I go in a room, what I am here after.

Well, if you've read this far you know by now that I am just one of those good old southern boys. Now if you plan to pay us a visit, I will give you some much needed suggestions, See what a bargain you'r getting, A tour guide would charge you much more than the price of this book.

1. Don't throw out the bacon grease… instructions to follow.
2. Just because you are able to manipulate on snow and ice, us southerners can't, so stay home the few days it snows in the south.
3. If you do run your car in a ditch, call Leroy and his buddy Bubba and they will bring a tow chain and a six pack. You just made their day.
4. Southerners don't read signs; just mountains, valleys, trees, rocks, etc.
5. Every southerner you meet will probably ask, "You ain't from around here, are you?"
6. You will hear a lot of ya'll and big ol' and stuff. Don't let it fret you none, it's our deep state language.
7. Try your best not to run over any of the good ole' boys driving down the middle of the road on their John Deere tractors. They ain't used to paved roads just yet.

8. Also, they will probably ignore any turn signals you give, so slow down.
9. Now about that bacon grease, if you don't cook with it, the food probably isn't worth eating.
10. Most of the satellite dishes in the south cost more than the house.
11. If there is a slight chance of snow, it is your sworn duty to go to the grocery store… has nothing to do with whether or not you need anything.
12. And if you get into any trouble, just remember, "he needed killing" is a valid defense in the south.

We aren't quite like the Beverly Hillbillies, I mean we have gotten to the point now where we know how to program a GPS, use cell phones to text and talk to friends and enjoy Facebook. We are high tech folks. But personally I'm still saving my confederate money.

WORLD EVENTS OF THE PAST 50 YEARS

1937   Shirley Temple was the #1 box office draw

The Hindenburg Helium Balloon Craft exploded killing all on board

1938   Disneys *Snow White* premiered

Howard Hughes circled the world by plane in 3 and 3/4 days.

Orson Welles created a panic by broadcasting *War Of The Worlds*

Joe E. Louis knocked out Max Schmeling to retain the heavyweight title

1939   Hitler invaded Poland and began WWII the Worlds Fair in New York had its opening debut

Gone With The Wind premiered with Clark Gable and Vivian Leigh

1940   German Luftwaffe relentlessly bombs London

Franklin Delano Roosevelt elected for unprecedented third term.

Womens nylon madness explodes sweeping the nation.

1941   December 6, 1941 A day that will live in infamy, Japan bombs Pearl Harbor and US goes to war.

Mount Rushmore is comleted and open to the public

Joe Dimaggio hits safely in 56 consecutive games for the Yankees.

1943   *Oklahoma* premiers on broadway

Penicillin was produced in mass quantities for the first time.

Band leader Harry James marries Betty Grable

Ole Blue Eyes became famous, known as Frank Swoonatra

1944   Allies invade the beaches of Normandy on D-Day
        Rodgers and Hammerstein win songwriting pulitizer.
        Eishenhower chosen as supreme allied commander
1945   Atomic bombs dropped on Nagasaki and Hiroshama ending
        WWII
        United Nations was founded
        Humphrey Bogart and Lauren Bacall were married
        B-25 bomber crashes into Empire State Building
        Marines raise the US flag on Iwo Jima
1946   Nazi leaders convicted of war crimes at the Nuremberg Trials
1947   India wins independence from Britain
        The house Un-American Activities Committee investigates
        Hollywood
        Jackie Robinson broke the color barrier in professional
        baseball
1948   Israel became a separate state
        Arthur Godfrey was the most listened to radio personality on
        air
        Soviet attempts to blockade Berlin was thwarted by US/
        British air drops
1949   Mao-Tse-Tungs's communist party establishes the Peoples
        Republic Of China
        South Pacific with Mary Martin became a broadway hit
        Bikinis debut in the United States
1950   United States enters the Korean War
        Liz Taylor and Conrad Hilton Jr. are married
        Brinks armored car robbed of 2.8 million dollars in Boston
        Hopalong Cassidy premiers on television as a series
1951   General Douglas Mcarthur fired by President Harry Truman
        Received an old soldiers welcome home from congress
        Citation was first race horse to win one million dollars
        Dean Martin and Jerry Lewis reached fame
        New York Giants win pennant

Back yard bomb shelters were being built in the neighborhoods

1952   Ike and Nixon retake White House after 20 years control by democrats

Gary Cooper receives an Oscar for his performance in *High Noon*

First hydrogen bomb test obliterates pacific island

Worst year ever for polio with 57,879 cases

First year of the 3-D movies

1953   Queen Elizabeth the second was crowned

I Love Lucy the top-rated television show

Jackie Bouvier married Senator Jack Kennedy

1954   Supreme Court rules against racial segregation in public schools

Marlon Brando won oscar for *On The Waterfront*

Marilyn Monroe weds Joe Dimaggio

Britain's Roger Bannister became worlds first sub-four minute miler

1955   First Geneva Summit took place

Lemans race car catapults into stands killing 80 people

Actor Jimmy Dean, dead at age 24 from auto crash

1956   *My Fair Lady* is big Broadway hit

Interstate highway construction begins

Prince Ranier and Grace Kelly wed

Elvis soars to success

1957   Soviets launch first space satellite, Sputnik, America in panic

West Side Story number one hit on Broadway

Evangelist Billy Graham holds crusade in Madison Square Garden

1958   Jayne Maynesfield married Mickey Hargitay

	Hula hoop becomes the rage to every kid on the block
1959	Castro rebels overthrow batista regime to control Cuba
	Pat Boone tops the charts
	Rock Hudson and Doris Day release *Pillow Talk*
1960	Jack Kennedy defeats Richard Nixon by a slim margin
	Birth control pills hit on open market
	Francis Gary Powers in U-2 spy plane shot down over Russia
	Grandma Moses turns 100
1961	East Germany constructs Berlin Wall
	Western films lead television ratings for fifth straight year
	Peace corps began
	US backed raid fails in Bay Of Pigs invasion to Cuba
	Alan Shepherd became first American in space
1962	Soviet missiles in Cuba create crisis
	Richard Burton and Liz Taylor film *Cleopatra*
	John Glenn returns from first US orbit of Earth
	The year of the twist
1963	President Kennedy assassinated by Lee Harvey Oswald
	The Mona Lisa visits the United States
	Martin Luther King Jr. holds *I Have A Dream Rally* in Washington D.C.
	Barbie is four years old and the most popular doll in toy history
1964	Lyndon Baines Johnson wins presidency in landslide
	English rock group known as Beatles take America by storm
	Earthquake in Alaska kills one hundred seventeen
	Bob Dylan ushers in a new era of folk music
1965	Race riots erupt in Los Angeles ghetto
	Ed White becomes first astronaut to walk in space
	Sonny and Cher top the billboard charts
	White boots, mini skirts and go go are the rage
1966	United States escalates air war in Vietnam
	Best selling novel is *Valley Of The Dolls*

Frank Sinatra marries for third time to actress Mia Farrow

1967   Moshe Dyan leads Israel in six day war with arabs

Dr. Christiaan Barnard performs first human heart transplant

Three astronauts die in shuttle space craft fire while still on pad

1968   Jackie Kennedy married Aristotle Onassis a greek shipping magnate

Robert Kennedy and Martin Luther King Jr. were both assassinated

1969   Buzz Armstrong and Alan Aldrin land on the moon

John Wayne got his first oscar for *True Grit*

Redford and Newman premiered *Butch Cassidy And The Sundance Kid*

Joe Namath led the New York Jets to the Super Bowl

Mini-skirts were the style of the country

1970   Four anti-war demonstrators were shot by national guardsman

1971   *All In The Family* was comedy sit com of the year

Police recapture Attica prison after inmate rioting causes death of 43

1972   Arabs kill eleven Israeli athletes at olympics

Bobby Fischer became first american to win world chess title

Nixon's visit opens up détente with China

World Trade Center towers are built

1973   Senator Sam Ervin presides over Watergate committee hearings

Secretariat became first triple crown winner in 25 years setting records that are still standing

Spiro Agnew resigns as Vice President amid allegations of tax fraud

Bruce Lee movies initiate the kung fu craze

1974   Nixon resigns as president elevating Gerald Ford to the presidency

The eight hundred mile Alaska pipeline begins

The arab oil embargo stretches gas pump lines

1975   US pulls out of Vietnam

First *Jaws* movie made

Pet rocks were the craze even though we thought it was home to some

1976   America celebrates it's bicentennial

Barbara Walters signs a one million dolar contract with ABC network

Jimmy Carter sworn in as 39th President of the United States

Bruce Jenner shatters olympic decathlon record

1977   *Roots* television series records unparalled ratings for the era

King Tut's treasures tour the US

Star Wars premiers and a new cult begins, known as the trekkies

1978   Dolly Parton awarded country music Entertainer of The Year

Mankind's first test tube baby was born

Jonestown, Guyana mass murder-suicides in cult leave 913 dead

Cassius Marcellus aka Clay Muhammed Ali wins world title for third time

1979   Iran holds fifty three US hostages at the American Embassy

Superman with Christopher Reeves premiers in theatres

Accident at Three Mile Island's nuclear plant sets off alarm

1980   Mt. Saint Helens volcano erupts in Washington State killing 60 people

The man america loved to hate Dallas's JR Ewing is top show for year

Voyager One photographs pictures of saturn

Rescue of iranian hostages fails

Beetles John Lennon is slain

1981   Ronald Reagan assassanation attempt, claimed later he forgot to duck

NASA launches re-usable space shuttle

Prince Charles weds Diana

Sandra Day O'conner becomes first female supreme court justice

1982   Barney Clark gets first artificial heart

British repulse Argentina claims to Falkland islands

Steven Spielberg premiers *ET*

1983   Terrorists truck bombing destroys marine barracks in Beirut killing 71

Cabbage patch dolls are the rage

Yankees owner George Steinbrenner fires Billy Martin for third time.

Soviets shoot down Korean Airlines flight killing all 264 passengers aboard

Sally Ride took the ride becoming Americas first female astronaut

1984   Ronald Reagan reelected for second term

Astronaut Bruce Mccandles floats in space untethered for first time

Walter Mondale chooses Geraldine Ferraro as his running mate

One million Ethopians starve to death in longest drought of century

Gymnast Mary Lou Retton wins Olympic Gold Medal

1985   Titanic is found two and one half miles deep in North Atlantic

Mexico City earthquake leaves 7000 dead, 30,000 homeless

Bill Cosby is televesions number one comedian

1986   Space shuttle Challenger explodes 74 seconds after liftoff killing all seven

Senate sessions are televised live for the first time

Chernobyl nuclear plant explosion in Soviet Union threatens 100,000 lives

Statue of Liberty celebrates 100 years on our shores

A new Plymouth or Dodge automobile fully maxed cost less than $8000.00

Printed in the United States
By Bookmasters